Langenscheidt

Sprachkurs für Faule
Deutsch 1

German for Lazy Learners

von Linn Hart und Paul Hawkins

Langenscheidt
München · Wien

Sprachkurs für Faule – Deutsch 1
Herausgegeben von der Langenscheidt-Redaktion

Autoren: Linn Hart und Paul Hawkins
Lektorat: Dr. Helen Galloway, Dr. Lutz Walther
Projektleitung: Andrea Freier, Susanne Meyer
Illustrationen: Linn Hart und Paul Hawkins (Innenteil), Elisa Sturm (S. 5), alle weiteren Illustrationen von Shutterstock.com
Design & Layout: Pia Stiegler, Friends Media Group GmbH, Augsburg
Umschlaggestaltung: Pia Stiegler und Elisa Sturm, Friends Media Group GmbH, Augsburg
Corporate Design Umschlag: KW43 BRANDDESIGN, Düsseldorf

Auf **www.langenscheidt.com/bonusmaterial** kannst du alle **MP3-Audiodateien** für den „Sprachkurs für Faule – Deutsch 1" herunterladen. Gib dazu bitte den Code **SFD325** ein.

All the mp3 audio files for "Sprachkurs für Faule – Deutsch 1" are available for download at **www.langenscheidt.com/bonusmaterial**. Please enter code **SFD325**.

www.langenscheidt.com

Satz: Pia Stiegler, Friends Media Group GmbH, Augsburg
Druck und Bindung: Druckerei C.H. Beck, Nördlingen

ISBN 978-3-468-28325-3

18010

Welcome to
"German for Lazy Learners"!

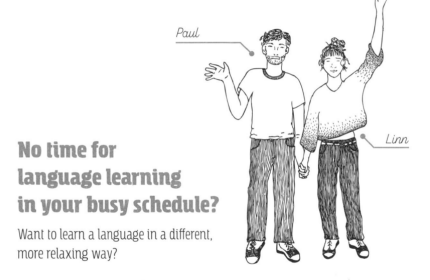

No time for language learning in your busy schedule?

Want to learn a language in a different, more relaxing way?

This is Paul and Linn,

Britain's most amazingly useless couple. They are clumsy, accident-prone, easily confused, slow to learn, quick to forget, and casually disastrous in just about every area of life that requires a brain. In spite of this (or maybe because of it), they are also happy.

This year, they have decided to go on a trip through the German-speaking world ... against the advice of their friends and family, who worry they will never see them again. Maybe you can help them survive ...

How it Works:

» Marvel at the **bizarre situations** Paul and Linn find themselves in on their trip through the German-speaking world.

» Help them out and give your German a boost with our **cool, bite-sized exercises** for improving your reading, listening and discovery skills.

» **Answers** and **translations** appear at the bottom of each page, and **transcripts of audio recordings** in the appendix.

Abbreviations and Symbols:

This exercise will take you approximately

◔ 3 minutes ◑ 5 minutes ◕ 7 minutes

🎧 This exercise is accompanied by an **audio recording** as an mp3 file. See page 2 for the **download code**.

m	masculine	*form*	formal
f	feminine	*inform*	informal
n	neuter	*e.g.*	zum Beispiel
m/f	masculine and feminine	*jmdn.*	jemanden
Pl	Plural	*s.o.*	someone
Sg	Singular	¨	addition of umlaut in plural form

Inhalt

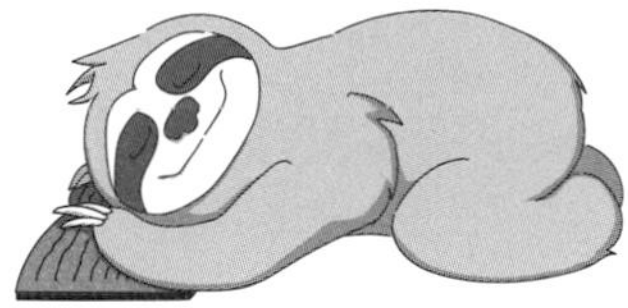

1 // The German alphabet and the English alphabet are written exactly the same, which is a handy bonus, given that there are about 10,000 more complicated things to deal with later. While there are some small variations in the pronunciation of some letters, these differences are still minor enough to fit into the rhythm of the alphabet song. You know the alphabet song? Of course you do!

Listen to the alphabet song in German, and hear how it differs from your own. Use the table below to sing along, karaoke style!

Track 1

A ah	**B** beh	**C** tseh	**D** deh	**E** eh
F eff	**G** geh	**H** hah	**I** ee	**J** yott
K kah	**L** el	**M** em	**N** en	**O** oh
P peh	**Q** kuh	**R** err	**S** ess	**T** teh
U oo	**V** fau	**W** veh	**X** iks	**Y** ypsilon
Z tsett				

2 // Some people will try to convince you that German sounds 'harsh'. Mostly these people will try to convince you by shouting otherwise lovely words at you, except angrily. "SCHMETTERLING!" they will shout, angrily. "See?" they will say afterwards, like the matter has now been settled forever, "It's so harsh!" When you speak German, you should not shout everything, angrily. Instead, you should talk at a normal volume, except keeping your mouth slightly tighter than normal. One tip is to imagine your mouth forming the shape of a large o or a small lowercase u when you open it.

Try it with the perfectly nice-sounding sentence below. Track 2

Der Schmetterling

Die Flügel des Schmetterlings flattern, wenn der Schmetterling vorbeiflattert.

The Butterfly

The wings of the butterfly flutter, as the butterfly flutters by.

3 // Of course, German does have one other important difference to English: the umlaut. These two little dots pop up occasionally to change the sound of the vowel, instantly turning boring, ordinary vowel letters into these cute little faces: o becomes the shocked face of ö, u becomes the very happy face of ü, and a becomes, well, this guy: ä. When writing on an English keyboard, they are expressed as *oe*, *ue*, and *ae*.

Listen to the examples. After listening once, the track will repeat, except with gaps for you to practise repeating the sounds. Track 3

Letter	Pronunciation	Example
ä	long **ehr** like **ai** in *hair*	**Käse** kehr-ze *cheese*
	short **e** like **e** in *let*	**Äpfel** epfel *apples*
ö	long **ur** like **ur** in *burn*	**Größe** grur-sse *size*
	short **uh** like **o** in *collapse*	**Können** kur-nen *ability*
ü	long **u** like French **u** in *sur*	**kühl** kewl *cool*
	short **u** like French **u** in *tu*	**Bürste** bewr-sste *brush*
äu	like **oy** in *boy*	**Läuse** loy-ze *lice*

4 // The German alphabet has all of the same consonants as the English, plus this wobbly guy ß. He's a lot of fun to draw (and dangerous... don't make him a B.) **The ß, pronounced es-zet, has the same sound as ss in English, i.e. Straße *street*, which on an English keyboard would be written Strasse.**

Have a look below at our handy reference to the pronunciation of some German consonant sounds which differ from their English counterparts.
After listening once, the track will repeat, except with gaps for you to practise repeating the sounds. Track 4

Letter	Pronunciation	Example
ch	like **ch** in Scottish *loch*	**Loch** lokh *hole*
j	like **y** in *yard*	**Jacke** ya-ke *jacket*
r	pronounced from back of throat	**Rand** rant *edge*
s	like **s** in *sign* or **z** in *zebra* or **sh** in *shop*	**Haus** howss *house* **Sonne** zon-ne *sun* **stark** shtaark *strong*
ß	like **ss** in *grass*	**Straße** shtraa-sse *street*
sch	like **sh** in *shop*	**Schule** shoo-le *school*
v	like **f** in *father*	**verloren** fer-lor-en *lost*
w	like **v** in *vase*	**Wasser** va-sse *water*
z	like **ts** in *tsar*	**Zahl** tsaal *number*

Airports require planning, organisation and good time-keeping. Naturally, Paul and Linn find them to be terrifying places. To give themselves the most hope of making it on time this morning, they set their alarm clock extra, extra early. Unfortunately, though, Paul immediately turned it off again because he was having an important dream where he was the Flying Cheese Ninja King of Dragon World.

1

Abgelenkt am Flughafen

Distracted at the Airport

1 // Luckily, their family show up to drive them to the airport, to increase the chances of them catching their flight by about 100%. It's also one last chance to drill some German 'goodbyes' into them before they go. Unfortunately, Aunt Dongleberry gets confused.

Which 'goodbye' is incorrect? Track 5

Bis bald!

Willkommen zurück!

Guten Flug!

SAY GOODBYE

Habt eine gute Reise!

AUF WIEDERSEHEN!

Right: Bis bald! *See you!* // Auf Wiedersehen! *Goodbye!* // Habt eine gute Reise! *Have a good trip!* // Guten Flug! *Have a good flight!*

Wrong: Willkommen zurück! *Welcome back!*

2 // Linn in particular has trouble with airport security procedures, given her charming tendency to store weird objects in her hair and clothes, and then immediately forget about them. **Can you name all the parts of her body which made the body scanner beep?**

die Taille	der Arm	der Fuß	die Brust	der Kopf	die Hand

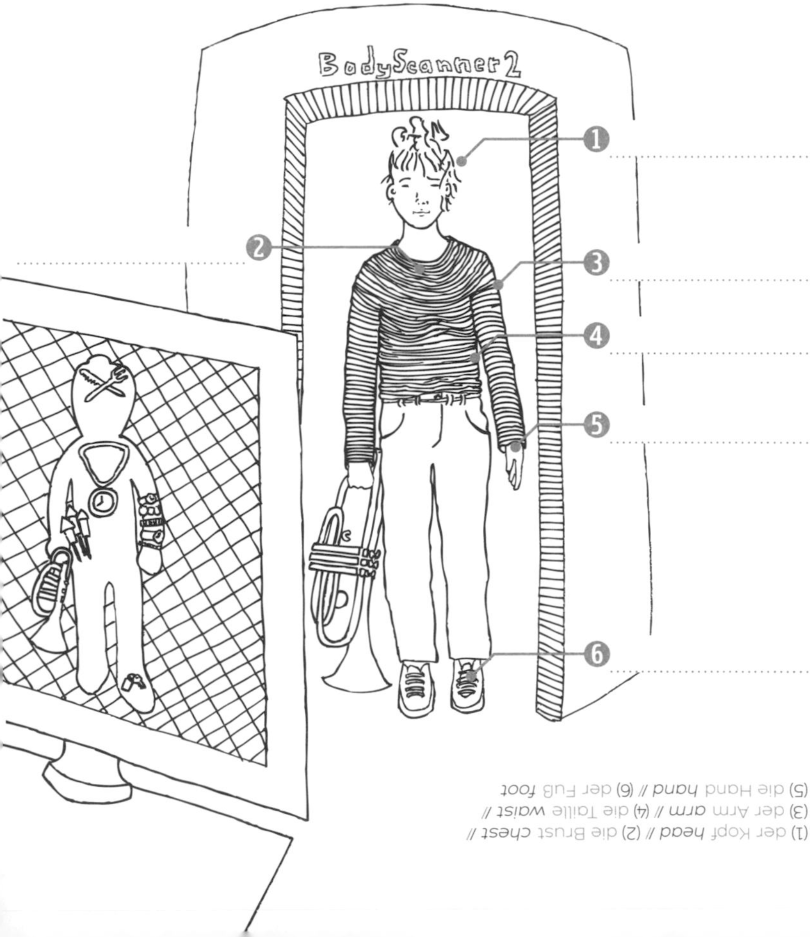

(1) der Kopf *head* // (2) die Brust *chest* // (3) der Arm *arm* // (4) die Taille *waist* // (5) die Hand *hand* // (6) der Fuß *foot*

3 // In all of the security check confusion, Paul and Linn have lost their travel plan. They decide to write themselves a new one out by hand, but mis-spell the names of every single country, city and attraction they hope to visit.

Can you help correct them?

OZTERREICH ....

DUTSCH SCHLAND ....

DIE SCHWIEZ ....

WIENA ....

DAS OCTUBERFEST ....

DER KÖLNER KARNEVIL ....

DER WALD DAS SCHWARZ IST ....

DER RHINE ....

DIE ALPENS ....

DIE NORDSEA ....

Österreich *Austria* // Deutschland *Germany* // die Schweiz *Switzerland* // Wien *Vienna* // das Oktoberfest *the Munich Beer Festival* // der Kölner Karneval *Cologne Carnival* // der Schwarzwald *the Black Forest* // der Rhein *the Rhine* // die Alpen *the Alps* // die Nordsee *the North Sea*

4 // Since all flights have been delayed (thanks to a strange incident involving an unexplained firework going off in the security area)**, Paul and Linn decide to play I spy. Unfortunately, there's not much to see, so it's a short game. In German, you play I spy with colours instead of the first letter of a word.** Track 6

Ich sehe was, was du nicht siehst, und das ist **blau.**

Ist es der (1) H................................?

Richtig! Du bist dran!

Okay! Ich sehe was, was du nicht siehst, und das ist **grün.**

Ist es (2) G................................?

Wow! Woher wusstest du das? Du bist wieder dran!

Ich sehe was, was du nicht siehst, und das ist **rot, gelb, blau, lila ...**

Oh mein Gott, ist es ein (3) R................................?

(1) (der) Himmel sky // (2) (das) Gras grass // (3) (der) Regenbogen rainbow

I spy with my little eye, something blue. // Is it the sky? // Correct! Your turn! // OK! I spy with my little eye, something green. // Is it grass? // Wow! How did you know?! You go again! // I spy with my little eye, something red, yellow, blue, violet ... // Oh my god, is it a rainbow?

5 // **After queuing up for the wrong flight several times** (they both thought the other one was leading), **Linn and Paul make it to the right gate. Unfortunately, the German-speaking airline employee has some bad news for them. Can you help her deliver the information ... politely?** Track 7

Schlange	fürchte ich	Vielen Dank	nächstes Jahr
es tut mir wirklich leid	Dienstag	Entschuldigung	

Oh je, (1).., **Ihnen das sagen zu müssen, aber Ihre Tickets sind leider für** (2).. **... nächstes Jahr. Ich würde Ihnen liebend gern helfen, aber ich kann da nichts tun,** (3)..........................**.** (4)..........................**, aber würde es Ihnen etwas ausmachen, aus der** (5).................................... **zu treten?** (6).................................... **. Wir freuen uns, Sie bald wiederzusehen. Also,** (7) .... **...**

(1) es tut mir wirklich leid *I'm really sorry* // (2) Dienstag *Tuesday* // (3) fürchte ich *I'm afraid* // (4) Entschuldigung *Sorry* // (5) Schlange *queue* // (6) Vielen Dank *Thank you* // (7) nächstes Jahr *next year*

Oh dear, I'm really sorry to have to tell you this, but unfortunately your tickets are for Tuesday ... next year. I would love to help you but there's nothing I can do, I'm afraid. Sorry, but would you mind getting out of the queue, please? Thank you. We look forward to seeing you again soon! Well, next year ...

6 // With a mere year to kill before their adventure begins, Paul and Linn decide to buy a German calendar so they can keep the excitement alive until their tickets are valid.

Unfortunately, they buy an English calendar by mistake, because it is hard to remember things. Never mind. Can you help them convert it into a German calendar by filling in the months in German? ⏱

~~Calendar~~ *Kalender*		
1	2	3
4	5	6
7	8	9
10	11	12

(1) Januar *January* // (2) Februar *February* // (3) März *March* // (4) April *April* // (5) Mai *May* // (6) Juni *June* // (7) Juli *July* // (8) August *August* // (9) September *September* // (10) Oktober *October* // (11) November *November* // (12) Dezember *December*

One year later, Paul and Linn have arrived in Berlin, the first destination of their trip. Hurray! However, in all the excitement of **successfully going on holiday**, they forget to collect their suitcases from the baggage carousel. 5 minutes later, the suitcases have been blown up, because German airport workers get bored too, you know.

Linn and Paul's first stop in Germany, then, is the shops ...

2

Orientierungslos im Kaufhaus

Lost in the Department Store

1 // Paul and Linn soon find the largest department store in Berlin: KaDeWe. Their entrance into the shop, however, is somewhat delayed, when they accidentally mistake a nice, semi-inebriated man on the floor for the doorman of a fancy shopping establishment that doesn't want to let time-wasters in.
Listen to the following conversation. Track 8

WHAT DOES JAKOB WANT?

- a *er will ihnen Geld geben*
- b *er will herausfinden, ob sie genug Geld haben, um einzukaufen*
- c *er will sie um Geld bitten*

Right: (c) er will sie um Geld bitten *he wants to ask them for money*
Wrong: (a) er will ihnen Geld geben *he wants to give them money* //
(b) er will herausfinden, ob sie genug Geld haben, um einzukaufen
he wants to find out if they have enough money to shop

2 // **Suddenly worried that they are not dressed fancily enough for the shop, Paul and Linn panic and run away. They realise quickly that they will need to get past "Jakob the Doorman" using some kind of incredible spy skills.**

Which skills below are famous spying skills? Circle them!

Track 9

Kleidung von jemandem ausleihen

besonders schnell Banjo spielen

schlafen

SICH VERSTECKEN

rennen

eine Ananas von jemandem borgen

HERUMSCHLEICHEN

Spies are good at: Herumschleichen *sneaking around* // Rennen *running* // Kleidung von jemandem ausleihen *borrowing someone else's clothes* // Sich verstecken *hiding*

Spies might have problems with: eine Ananas von jemandem borgen *borrowing someone else's pineapple* // besonders schnell Banjo spielen *playing the banjo really fast* // Schlafen *sleeping*

3 // Once inside the store, Paul and Linn immediately lose each other. Luckily, it's not the first time it's happened (this week)**, and they have a foolproof system prepared: Linn goes to find the nearest information point, while Paul waits in the nearest ball pit to hear his name announced over the store's Tannoy® system. They need to ask directions. Can you find some useful words for them?**

geradeaus | rechts | links

Richtung | rückwärts | umkehren | vorwärts

I	Y	V	O	N	S	N	H	N	S	W	W	R
G	M	R	V	H	K	V	V	S	H	C	Z	U
E	X	I	G	R	M	F	O	S	M	X	A	K
R	S	C	P	Y	L	C	R	F	Z	U	C	V
A	M	H	O	Q	T	Y	W	L	M	F	N	M
D	A	T	K	S	R	X	Ä	R	Y	K	J	V
E	L	U	M	K	E	H	R	E	N	U	N	A
A	S	N	Z	D	X	Y	T	C	Y	A	T	K
U	O	G	J	E	N	U	S	H	R	T	I	E
S	R	Ü	C	K	W	Ä	R	T	S	T	T	W
L	Q	U	V	L	I	N	K	S	A	Q	G	U

Across: umkehren *to turn around* // rückwärts *backwards* // links *left*

Down: geradeaus *straight ahead* // Richtung *direction* // vorwärts *forwards* // rechts *right*

4 // **After reuniting, they make a list of all the things they need to replace from their suitcases. They decide to split the list up into two categories, partly in case they accidentally lose each other again, and partly because Linn feels that she too deserves some time in the ball pit. Paul will buy clothes for the top half of their bodies, Linn for the bottom half. Which items go on which list?**

T-Shirt Hemd Hose Krawatte

BH Rock Shorts Socken

Strumpfhose Schmuck Schuhe Unterhose

Klamotten für den Oberkörper	Klamotten für den Unterkörper

Items for the top half: das T-Shirt *T-shirt* // das Hemd *shirt* // die Krawatte *tie* // der BH *bra* // der Schmuck *jewellery*

Items for the bottom half: die Unterhose *pants* // die Hose *trousers* // der Rock *skirt* // die Socke(n) *sock(s)* // die Shorts *shorts* // der Schuh/die Schuhe *shoe(s)* // die Strumpfhose *tights*

5 // Unfortunately, it is only when they get to the cashier that Paul and Linn remember that their wallets were in their forgotten and now irreparably exploded suitcases. Ah.

They experiment with cursing angrily, like they see less happy people do sometimes. Which exclamations below are real German phrases, and which are not? (Mind the traps!)

right wrong

❶ ☐ ☐ Verdammte Scheiße!

❷ ☐ ☐ BLUTIGE HÖLLE!

❸ ☐ ☐ Wie dumm ist das denn?!

❹ ☐ ☐ Jesus Christus!

❺ ☐ ☐ HIMMELHERRGOTT!

Right: (1) Verdammte Scheiße! *Damnit! (Literally: Damned shit!)* // (3) Wie dumm ist das denn?! *How stupid is that?!* // (5) Himmelherrgott! *Heavens above!*

Wrong: (2) // (4)

6 // After checking with the cashier if the shop accepts buttons, smiles or compliments as a form of currency (it doesn't)**, Paul and Linn realise they will need to come back another time.**

Annoyed, the cashier decides to write them a list of all the items' names so they can do the same shopping online later instead, and so he doesn't have to deal with them again. Can you match up the pairs below?

die Zahnbürste underwear

das Deo shower gel

die Zahnpasta earphones

die Unterwäsche phone charger

die Sonnenbrille toothbrush

das Duschgel hair brush

das Handyladegerät sunglasses

DIE HAARBÜRSTE PARTY HAT

der Kopfhörer toothpaste

DAS PARTYHÜTCHEN DEODORANT

die Zahnbürste *toothbrush* // das Deo *deodorant* // die Zahnpasta *toothpaste* // die Unterwäsche *underwear* // die Sonnenbrille *sunglasses* // das Duschgel *shower gel* // das Handyladegerät *phone charger* // die Haarbürste *hair brush* // der Kopfhörer *earphones* // das Partyhütchen *party hat*

While waiting for some money to be wired to them, Linn and Paul get a very cool-sounding website recommended to them where they can ask to stay on strangers' couches for free. They search through dozens of profiles, before settling on a girl called Luzie, who looks super cool, interesting and fun. They send her a nice message, and she agrees to host them. Woohoo!

3

Gelangweilt mit einer Fremden

Bored with a Stranger

1 // **Unfortunately, they somehow seem to have misjudged the excitingness of Luzie's online presence by around 100%. Not long after she has invited them into her entirely beige home, Paul and Linn realise she is probably the world's most boring person.**

Listen to the following conversation. Track 10

Which boring industry does Luzie most likely work in?

(a) *Landwirtschaft* (b) *Finanzsektor* (c) *Weltraumforschung*

Wrong: (a) Landwirtschaft *agriculture* // (c) Weltraumforschung *space exploration*

Right: (b) Finanzsektor *finance*

2 // Luzie shows them around her apartment, which is a pro-actively dull interior space of interconnected boring rectangles. Indeed, only one or two objects in each room give any clue as to what the room is used for.

Can you guess all of the room names, based on the few objects Paul and Linn spot inside them?

(das) Sofa, (der) Fernseher, (die) Hausschuhe	das W..
(der) Ofen, (der) Kühlschrank, (das) gerahmte Foto eines gekochten Eis	die K..
(die) Dusche, (das) Waschbecken, (die) Gummiente	das B..
(das) Bett, (der) Schlafanzug, (die) Schnarchschiene	das S..

das Sofa *sofa* // der Fernseher *television* // die Hausschuhe *slippers* //
das Wohnzimmer *living room/lounge* // der Ofen *oven* // der Kühlschrank *fridge* //
das gerahmte Foto eines gekochten Eis *the framed phoho of a boiled egg* //
die Küche *kitchen* // die Dusche *shower* // das Waschbecken *sink* //
die Gummiente *rubber duck* // das Badezimmer *bathroom* // das Bett *bed* //
der Schlafanzug *pyjamas* // die Schnarchschiene *anti-snoring mouthguard* //
das Schlafzimmer *bedroom*

3 // Thankfully, the tour soon ends (well, after about 10,000 years, subjectively). **Paul and Linn take a seat in the room with the fridge and the oven in it, while Luzie cooks. They try desperately to get something interesting out of her, but only dig themselves deeper into a boredom hole. Which incredibly fun questions fit with which incredibly boring answers?** Track 11

① *Hast du Geschwister?*	ICH MAG KEINE TIERE. ⓐ
② *Was ist dein Sternzeichen?*	ES IST MIR UNANGENEHM, ÜBER MEIN LIEBESLEBEN ZU SPRECHEN. ⓑ
③ *Hast du ein Haustier?*	4 JAHRE, 8 MONATE, 3 WOCHEN, 5 TAGE, 13 STUNDEN UND 6 MINUTEN, GLAUBE ICH. ⓒ
④ *Bist du gegen irgendwas allergisch?*	ICH KENNE MEIN STERNZEICHEN NICHT. ⓓ
⑤ *Hast du einen Freund?*	ICH HABE KEINE GESCHWISTER. ⓔ
⑥ *Wie lange wohnst du schon hier?*	LEIDER NICHT, ICH NIESE GERN. ⓕ

1 e // 2 d // 3 a // 4 f // 5 b // 6 c

Do you have brothers or sisters? – I have no siblings. // What is your star sign? – I don't know my star sign. // Do you have a pet? – I don't like animals. // Are you allergic to anything? – Unfortunately not, I like to sneeze. // Do you have a boyfriend? – I'm not comfortable talking about my love life. // How long have you lived here? – 4 years, 8 months, 3 weeks, 5 days, 13 hours and 6 minutes, I guess.

4 // **Even before they have finished eating dinner** (boiled potatoes with celery and bread), **Paul and Linn run out of things to say entirely. An impending time-bomb of social awkwardness starts ticking ... from which only small talk can save them.** **They need help ... urgently! Can you find the five words for mindless, generic topics of conversation below?**

das Wetter · der Sport · das Fernsehen · Donald Trump · die Arbeit

Y	Y	L	W	U	H	N	K	Y	B	M	V	D
J	A	D	M	K	I	A	L	U	O	Z	T	O
I	D	A	S	F	E	R	N	S	E	H	E	N
E	S	S	T	R	W	S	L	U	R	X	Q	A
M	F	W	E	W	D	F	J	Y	P	J	L	L
Z	R	E	M	K	M	A	K	G	D	J	O	D
Y	D	T	G	V	V	S	P	N	A	P	G	T
Z	U	T	L	V	Y	Q	F	X	S	F	O	R
D	I	E	A	R	B	E	I	T	E	I	F	U
D	E	R	S	P	O	R	T	G	S	V	Q	M
T	V	B	Z	F	Q	Y	I	W	S	T	D	P

Across: das Fernsehen *television* // die Arbeit *work* // der Sport *sport*

Down: das Wetter *weather* // Donald Trump

5 // **Unfortunately, Luzie is able to deflect all small-talk topics with her military-grade lack of interestingness. As dessert arrives** (tofu ice-cream, served warm)**, the awkward** (and flavourless) **silence is almost unbearable.**

Paul and Linn try to think of excuses to go to bed early. Can you find the German equivalents? Which word doesn't have a partner?

Kopfschmerzen *smelly farts*

Schönheitsschlaf the phone rings

Bauchschmerzen **tiredness**

Außerirdische wanting to get up early

früh aufstehen wollen having a cold

MÜDIGKEIT ***TUMMY ACHE***

das Telefon klingelt

STINKENDE FÜRZE **HEADACHE**

eine Erkältung haben aliens

Equivalents: die Kopfschmerzen *headache* // die Bauchschmerzen *tummy ache* // Außerirdische *aliens* // früh aufstehen wollen *wanting to get up early* // die Müdigkeit *tiredness* // das Telefon klingelt *the phone rings* // stinkende Fürze *smelly farts* // eine Erkältung haben *having a cold*

Word without a partner: der Schönheitsschlaf *beauty sleep*

6 // **Paul and Linn start yawning furiously, using all of their acting skills to convince Luzie that they simply must go to bed right now** (it's 6.43pm). **In fact, they are planning to enjoy the benefits of having no luggage ... by climbing out of the window and legging it.**
Given their plan, which of the following pre-going-to-bed statements are suspicious and which are not suspicious? ⏱

	Not Suspicious	Suspicious	
❶	☐	☐	GUTE NACHT!
❷	☐	☐	Ich bin soooo müde!
❸	☐	☐	*Viel Glück mit allem!*
❹	☐	☐	*In welchem Stockwerk sind wir?*
❺	☐	☐	Wo ist das nächste Hotel? Hast du eine Taxinummer?
❻	☐	☐	**BIS MORGEN! SCHLAF GUT!**

Not suspicious: (1) Gute Nacht! *Good night!* //
(2) Ich bin soooo müde! *I am soooo tired!* //
(6) Bis Morgen! Schlaf gut! *See you tomorrow! Sleep well!*
Suspicious: (3) Viel Glück mit allem! *Good luck with everything!* //
(4) In welchem Stockwerk sind wir? *Which floor are we on?* //
(5) Wo ist das nächste Hotel? Hast du eine Taxinummer?
Where is the nearest hotel? Do you have a taxi number?

After their recent adventures on the expansive plains of cosmic boringness, Paul and Linn feel a newfound urgency to make friends. They look online for meet-ups and discover a **Stammtisch** for expats who want to practise their German whilst getting drunk. Perfect! They immediately latch on to a group of their fellow Brits at the bar, who don't protest, for fear of seeming rude.

4 Ein zunehmend schwieriger Pub-Besuch

An Increasingly Tricky Pub Visit

1 // Normally in Germany, German people pay for their drinks at the end of the night. Normally in the world, however, British people do the exact same thing they do in Britain, except louder.

Immediately, then, a familiar politeness battle breaks out in front of Paul and Linn about whose "round" it is.

Listen to the following conversation.

Track 12

WHAT DOES ONE OF THE FRIENDS TELL THE OTHER ONES?

a *Ihr habt schon Runden bezahlt.*

b *Ich habe heute eine Beförderung bekommen.*

c *Ich habe eh mehr Geld als ihr.*

Right: (a) Ihr habt schon Runden bezahlt. *You've already paid for rounds.*
Wrong: (b) Ich habe heute eine Beförderung bekommen. *I got a promotion today.* //
(c) Ich habe eh mehr Geld als ihr. *I have more money than you anyway.*

2 // **Paul and Linn pay close attention to the exchange with the bartender to try and learn correctly how to incorrectly order beer in Germany. However, they get a bit muddled up. Can you put the words of each sentence between the bartender and the customer into the correct order** (including the punctuation!)**?**

1. sechs | kann | ich | Bier | Entschuldigung | , | bekommen | bitte | ?

   ....

2. sehr | Bitte | . | noch | sonst | es | Darf | etwas | sein | ?

   ....

3. **danke | , | Nein | .**

   ....

4. *Euro / vierzig / Das / und / dann / siebzehn / macht / Cents / .*

   ....

5. sind | Hier | zwanzig | .

   ....

6. ist | dein | : | Wechselgeld | Hier | sechzig | zwei | und | Euro | . | Cents

   ....

7. *so / ! / Stimmt /*

   ....

(1) Entschuldigung, kann ich bitte sechs Bier bekommen? *Excuse me, can I please get six beers?* // (2) Bitte sehr. Darf es sonst noch etwas sein? *There you are. Can I get you anything else?* // (3) Nein, danke. *No thanks.* // (4) Das macht dann siebzehn Euro und vierzig Cents. *That'll be seventeen euros and forty cents.* // (5) Hier sind zwanzig. *There's twenty.* // (6) Hier ist dein Wechselgeld: zwei Euro und sechzig Cents. *There's your two euros and sixty cents change.* // (7) Stimmt so! *Keep the change.*

3 // **During their first, second and third free beers, Linn and Paul begin to notice** (incorrectly) **that their German skills are improving** (they're not), **despite no new information having entered their brains.**

What else could explain this phenomenon? Put the states of drunkenness below in order of time, from earliest to latest.

(a) eingeschlafen / bewusstlos

(b) nüchtern / durstig

(c) betrunken / besoffen / stockbesoffen / hackedicht / völlig zugedröhnt

(d) verkatert / reuevoll

(e) lustig / beschwipst

1 2 3 4 5

1b // 2e // 3c // 4a // 5d

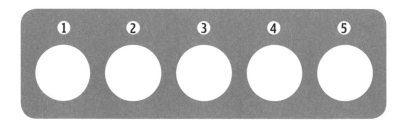

(a) nüchtern/durstig *sober/thirsty* // (b) lustig/beschwipst *merry/tipsy* //
(c) betrunken/besoffen/stockbesoffen/hackedicht/völlig zugedröhnt
drunk/pissed/smashed/wasted/hammered //
(d) eingeschlafen/bewusstlos *asleep/unconscious* //
(e) verkatert/reuevoll *hungover/regretful*

4 // After their third round of free beers, Paul and Linn decide to find out if other kinds of alcohol also have the same language-improving abilities (they don't). **However, the names of all the drinks behind the bar seem to have become mysteriously blurry and hard to read ... Can you figure out the names of all of these popular drinks... with their correct articles?!**

muR ....

inG ....

inwißeWe ....

Reinwot ....

adoWk ....

khWsiy ....

(der) Rum *rum* // (der) Gin *gin* // (der) Weißwein *white wine* //
(der) Rotwein *red wine* // (der) Wodka *vodka* // (der) Whisky *whisky*

5 // **The 4 free drinks inside Paul and Linn have taken control of the decision-making process: they have decided that Paul, Linn and everyone else in the pub would like to drink more drinks. As they realise it is their round, however, they simultaneously realise the stubborn non-existence of their wallets. Ah.**

They need money. Can you translate the different options below? Track 13

betteln

....

drucken

printing

stehlen

....

GELD

(als Geschenk) erhalten

....

BORGEN/AUSLEIHEN

....

tauschen

....

betteln *begging* // stehlen *stealing* // borgen/ausleihen *borrowing* //
tauschen *trading* // (als Geschenk) erhalten *receiving (as a gift)* // drucken *printing*

6 // **At that moment, a wealthy Nigerian prince appears! With miraculous timing, he tells them an** (almost) **unbelievable story: not only is he the heir to a vast fortune, he needs help getting it out of his country ... and is offering a huge reward!**

Wow! Linn and Paul immediately accept his offer to help. He hands them a list of the information he needs. But one item is a bit out of place. Which one?

- O ihre Namen
- O Telefonnummern
- O Adresse
- O Unterhosengröße
- O Bankverbindung
- O Geheimnummer

ihre Namen **their names** // Telefonnummern **phone numbers** // Adresse **address** // Unterhosengröße **underpants size** (out of place) // Bankverbindung **bank details** // Geheimnummer **pin number**

While they wait for their vast fortune to arrive, Linn and Paul go to a museum to kill some time. Unfortunately, they are incredibly hungover and tired. Very quickly, they fall asleep in the museum, right in the middle of the 'sleeping people' exhibit, so the security guards don't notice them when they lock the building.

They wake up in the dark ...

5

Schreck im Museum

Scared in the Museum

1 // **Paul and Linn turn on the torch functions on their phones, and look around to see the sleeping statues all around them. They realise it is night-time, and they are locked in the museum!**

Which four signs might help them to find their way out?

	right	wrong	
1	☐	☐	Ausgang
2	☐	☐	EINGANG
3	☐	☐	Toiletten
4	☐	☐	Souvenirladen
5	☐	☐	RAUCHEN VERBOTEN!
6	☐	☐	Nicht berühren!
7	☐	☐	Notausgang
8	☐	☐	GARDEROBE
9	☐	☐	*Ein Post-it mit einer Telefonnummer und der Bemerkung: „Sind Sie eingeschlossen worden? Rufen Sie Stefan an!“*

Signs that might help: (1) Exit // (2) Entrance // (7) Fire Exit // (9) A post-it note with a phone number that says, „Have you been locked in? Call Stefan!"
Signs that might not help: (3) Toilets // (4) Gift Shop // (5) No smoking! // (6) Do not touch! // (8) Cloakroom

2 // Paul challenges Linn to tell a ghost story ... in German! They put their phone torches underneath their faces, pointing upwards. In her excitement, she sometimes says the opposite of the German word she means. These incorrect words have been crossed out. Can you fill in what she should have said in the gaps below? Track 14

schwarze | kalten | stür-mische | dunkle

Es war eine (1) ~~helle~~ ……………………

und (2) ~~windstille~~ …………………… Nacht.

Das Mädchen war allein in einem (3) ~~warmen~~

…………………… Haus. Plötzlich hörte sie

das Geräusch von Schritten! Sie drehte sich

um und sah die Ursache des Geräusches: eine

(4) ~~weiße~~ …………………… Katze. Sie

erinnerte sich plötzlich wieder daran,

dass sie der Katze vor einer Weile Schuhe

angezogen hatte, weil ihr langweilig war.

Somit war alles wieder in Ordnung. Ende.

(1) dunkle *dark* // (2) stürmische *stormy* // (3) kalten *cold* // (4) schwarze *black*

It was a dark and stormy night. The girl was alone in a cold house. Suddenly, she heard the sound of footsteps! She turned around and saw the source of the noise: a black cat. She suddenly remembered that she had put shoes on the cat's feet earlier, because she had been bored. Then everything was fine again. The end.

3 // After a few hours of telling rubbish ghost stories to each other, Paul's and Linn's phones die. Suddenly, getting out of the museum seems entirely complicated. Realising that mobile phones (with enough battery) **are the solution to all life's problems, they start looking for a socket to charge them. While they look, can you find all of the useful phone-charging words below?**

Kabel | Elektrizität | Steckdose | Stecker | aufladen | Batterie

O	A	B	W	R	W	T	B	H	O	G	K	D
U	R	N	T	W	R	B	T	M	H	T	K	E
J	W	S	Z	S	N	K	U	C	Y	U	A	G
D	U	A	M	T	B	A	O	O	H	D	B	E
U	S	U	X	E	A	S	T	E	C	K	E	R
M	F	F	R	C	T	I	X	S	C	J	L	Ä
A	E	L	E	K	T	R	I	Z	I	T	Ä	T
V	T	A	W	D	E	N	S	K	Y	M	M	W
H	Q	D	R	O	R	U	Q	G	I	Y	J	D
R	H	E	Q	S	I	X	Y	Z	U	Q	B	E
R	X	N	X	E	E	N	K	P	X	I	C	K

Across: (der) Stecker *plug* // (die) Elektrizität *electricity*

Down: aufladen *to charge* // (die) Steckdose *socket* // (die) Batterie *battery* // (das) Kabel *cable*

4 // In the darkness, Paul and Linn crawl in opposite directions, feeling for the edges of the room so they can find a socket. Suddenly, Paul's hand touches another person's hand. The owner of the hand screams. Then Paul screams. Then Linn screams, further away.

The owner of the hand shouts out lots of questions. He seems to think he is communing with ghosts. Can you complete the questions he shouts?

1	Wann	... bist du? Kenne ich dich?	a
2	Warum	... kann das sein?!	b
3	Wer	... passiert hier?	c
4	Wie	... bist du gestorben? Ist das lange her?	d
5	Was	... bist du nicht tot?	e

1 d // 2 e // 3 a // 4 b // 5 c

When did you die? Was it long ago? // Why are you not dead? // Who are you? Do I know you? // How is this possible?! // What is happening here?

5 // **Paul and Linn realise the terrified man in front of them is the security guard, Stefan. They explain that they were locked in the museum; he explains that he thought that they were strange museum ghosts, trying to haunt him** (again).

He explains what happened. Listen to the following conversation.

Track 15

How often do people get locked in?

a *geradezu jede Nacht*

b *ziemlich oft*

c *fast nie*

Right: (c) fast nie *almost never*

Wrong: (a) geradezu jede Nacht *literally every single night* // (b) ziemlich oft *quite often*

6 // As Stefan leads them out of the museum, they accidentally set the burglar alarm off. Flashing lights and loud noises fill the museum, clearly trying to scare off any potential criminals (or, indeed, ghosts)**.**

What kind of people do they expect to arrive next? Match the words and translations.

Ärzte *teachers*
Polizisten criminals
Soldaten firefighters
Feuerwehrleute celebrities
Bankangestellte soldiers
LEHRER *DOCTORS*
Prominente *feminists*
Kriminelle bankers
Feministinnen *police officers*

They expect: Polizisten *police officers*
They don't expect: Ärzte *doctors* // Soldaten *soldiers* // Feuerwehrleute *firefighters* // Bankangestellte *bankers* // Lehrer *teachers* // Prominente *celebrities* // Kriminelle *criminals* // Feministinnen *feminists*

Unfortunately, despite all the best efforts of their new friend, The Prince, all of their money somehow ends up in the hands of Nigerian email scammers instead. What a mystery!

Without funds, Paul and Linn decide to look for a job. Luckily, they find a website designed for cash-strapped travellers, offering manual, low-paid exploitation in exchange for selfie opportunities. Can you help them apply?

6

Ein Notfalljob
An Emergency Job

1 // **Browsing through the website, Paul and Linn try to find jobs that don't require special training, certificates, qualifications, expertise, or a sensible personality trait of any kind.**

Can you organise the jobs below into jobs they can apply for, and jobs they can't?

	right	wrong			right	wrong	
1	☐	☐	Hundeausführer(in)	5	☐	☐	BABYSITTER(IN)
2	☐	☐	Rechtsanwalt/-anwältin	6	☐	☐	Kapitän eines Luftkissenbootes
3	☐	☐	INGENIEUR(IN)	7	☐	☐	Obstpflücker(in)
4	☐	☐	Barkeeper(in)	8	☐	☐	Hirnchirurg(in)

Possible jobs: (1) *dog walker* // (4) *bartender* // (5) *babysitter* // (7) *fruit picker*
Impossible jobs: (2) *lawyer* // (3) *engineer* // (6) *hovercraft pilot* // (8) *brain surgeon*

2 // By amazing luck, Paul and Linn see two positions advertised at a piglet sanctuary. It sounds like a dream job, so they start applying for it immediately, before somebody else can grab this rare opportunity!

What should they do? Listen to the options and pick the correct formulation!

Track 16

1. a ☐ ihr Interesse ausdrücken — b ☐ ihre Fantasien ausdrücken
2. a ☐ Suppe kochen — b ☐ Kontakt herstellen
3. a ☐ Weihnachtskarten verschicken — b ☐ eine Bewerbung abschicken
4. a ☐ sich um den Job bewerben — b ☐ sich um die Möglichkeit einer Bewerbung um einen Job bewerben
5. a ☐ Netflixen und Chillen — b ☐ höflich und professionell sein

They should: 1 a express their interest // 2 b make contact // 3 b send an application // 4 a apply for the job // 5 b be polite and professional

They should not: 1 b express their fantasies // 2 a make soup // 3 a send some Christmas cards // 4 b apply for the chance to apply for the job // 5 a netflix and chill

3 // **After bringing their CVs on holiday with them, Paul and Linn decide to make some photocopies before they send them off. This is all surprisingly responsible behaviour for them. To restore balance to the universe, they then put their CVs into a shredder, believing it to be a photocopier.** (Balance restored.)

Now they must write new CVs from scratch. What should they include? Track 17

Namen ihrer besten Referenzen

Schulbildung

Zeugnisse und Zertifikate

KONTAKTDATEN

Hobbys und Interessen

NAMEN IHRER PROFESSIONELLSTEN HAUSTIERE

frühere Beschäftigungsverhältnisse

Include: Schulbildung *education* // Hobbys und Interessen *hobbies and interests* // frühere Beschäftigungsverhältnisse *previous employment* // Kontaktdaten *contact details* // Namen ihrer besten Referenzen *names of their best references* // Zeugnisse und Zertifikate *qualifications and certificates*

Not include: Namen ihrer professionellsten Haustiere *names of their most professional pets*

4 // **Next, Paul and Linn each write an "Anschreiben", the opening letter that accompanies most job applications, which introduces them and says why they want the job. Not only do they unknowingly fill it with every cliché imaginable, they both write exactly the same letter.** **Can you fill in the gaps?**

- leidenschaftlich gern Musik
- über den Tellerrand schaut
- selbstständig
- bewerbe mich um

"Ich (1) .... die Stelle des Schweinchen-Babysitters. Das ist genau der Job, den ich suche! Ich bin eine kreative Person, die (2) .... Ich bin (3) .... , aber auch ein guter Teamplayer. Ich bin sehr unabhängig. In meiner Freizeit höre ich (4) .... , sehe Filme und treffe Freunde, genau wie jeder andere auch. Ich freue mich, von Ihnen zu hören!"

(1) bewerbe mich um // (2) über den Tellerrand schaut // (3) selbstständig // (4) leidenschaftlich gern Musik

"I am applying for the role of Piglet Babysitter. This is exactly the job I am looking for! I am a creative person who thinks outside the box. I am a self-starter, who is also a good team-player. I am very independently-minded. In my spare time, I am passionate about listening to music, watching films and socialising with friends, just like everybody else. I look forward to hearing from you!"

5 // After sending in their CVs and cover letters, Paul and Linn get a WhatsApp message back about the job they applied for. Or, at least, about *a* job they applied for ...

There seems to be some kind of a mix-up. Whose fault do you think it is? ◑

Sind das Paul ... und Linn?

Ja! Hallo!

Ähm, ich glaube, ihr habt mir zwei Kopien desselben Lebenslaufs geschickt. Ist das richtig?

Ja! Wir haben nur andere Namen! Geht es um den Job im Schweinchen-Tierheim?

Äh ..., naja, nicht wirklich. Sagt mal, habt ihr die Anzeige richtig gelesen, bevor ihr euch beworben habt?

Nicht wirklich! Bekommen wir den Job?!

Ich denke, ihr solltet die Anzeige noch mal lesen und euch dann bei mir melden ...

It's Paul and Linn's fault.

Is this Paul ... and Linn? // Yes! Hi! // Um, I think you sent me two copies of the same CV. Is that right? // Yes! Except we have different names! Is it about the piglet sanctuary job? // Errr, well, not really. Tell me, did you read the advert properly before you applied? // Not really! Did we get the job?! // I think you'd better read the advert again and get back to me ...

6 // **Paul and Linn head back to the jobs website to look for the piglet sanctuary listing, this time noticing a worryingly mixed bag of reviews from other travellers.**

Can you match the reviews to the emojis below? Track 18

1. Ich bin wütend! Es ist kein Tierheim!
2. Ich bin so traurig! Die armen Schweinchen!
3. Das ist urkomisch! Das kann nicht wahr sein!
4. Oh mein Gott, nee! Käse aus Schweinemilch?!
5. Ich liebe es! Schweinekäse ist mein Favorit!
6. Ich mag Schweinekäse (lieber als Wombat-Joghurt)

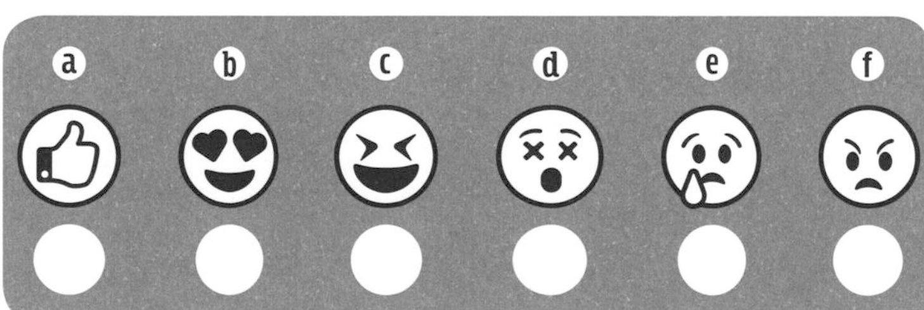

1 f // 2 e // 3 c // 4 d // 5 b // 6 a

I'm furious! It's not a sanctuary! // I'm so sad! The poor piglets! // This is hilarious! It can't be real! // Oh my god, no! Cheese from pig's milk?! // I love it! Pig cheese is my favourite! // I like pig cheese (more than wombat yoghurt)

After a few months of selfie-earning exploitation in the saddest piglet sanctuary imaginable (great cheese, though), Linn and Paul decide to begin their travels in earnest by throwing cash at the problem of transport. They decide to buy the most clichéd vehicle imaginable, a VW camper van, in the hope that it will kick-start an instantly classic adventure.

7

Eine Panne

A Breakdown

1 // Paul and Linn decide to buy the camper van, and try to haggle for it in German. Unfortunately, they've forgotten how to use numbers.

Listen to the conversation: Can you fill in the numbers you hear?

Track 19

(1)............................ .

(2)............................ ?

Äh ..., okay ...

dann (3)............................ ?

(4)............................ !

Oh, äh ... wow.
Äh ... nein, soviel kann ich nicht annehmen.

(5)............................ !

Nein.

Wie wäre es mit

(6)............................ ?

Ähm, okay. Also.

Sagen wir (7)............................ .
Abgemacht?

Abgemacht!

(1) 2.000 // (2) 2.999 // (3) 3.000 // (4) 17.968 // (5) 6 // (6) 3.500 // (7) 3.501

2000 // 2999? // Er, ok ... 3000, then? // 17,968! // Oh, er ... wow. Er ... no, I couldn't take that much. // 6! // No. // How about 3500? // Um, ok. Right. Let's say 3501. Deal? // Deal!

2 // They pay for the vehicle. Afterwards, they decide to inspect it for major problems so they can decide in hindsight whether it was a good idea to have already bought it. It's at this moment that they notice, for example, that there are some wheels missing.

What else should they check before they start driving it?

der Sitz	die Tür	der Auspuff	die Stoßstange	der Scheinwerfer

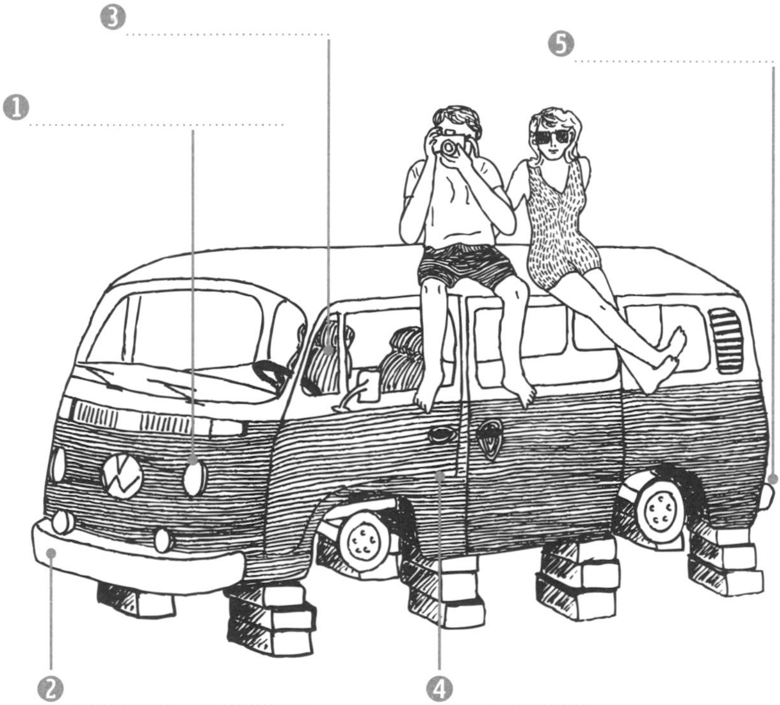

(1) der Scheinwerfer *headligths* // (2) die Stoßstange *bumper* // (3) der Sitz *seat* // (4) die Tür *door* // (5) der Auspuff *exhaust*

3 // **After noticing a few more minor faults with the van** (broken tail light, cracked wing mirror, missing engine)**, Linn and Paul realise they'll need to spend a bit more money on it to make it "roadworthy". Luckily, they don't mind since they got it for such a great price with their excellent haggling.**

Which kind of professional do they need to haggle with next ... and which building will they find them in? Join up the two correct answers!

❶ *ein(e) Automechaniker(in)*	**DIE KIRCHE** ⓐ
❷ *ein(e) Bäcker(in)*	**DER BLUMENLADEN** ⓑ
❸ *ein(e) Florist(in)*	**DIE BÄCKEREI** ⓒ
❹ *ein Priester*	**DIE AUTOWERKSTATT** ⓓ
❺ *ein(e) Schauspieler(in)*	**DIE BANK** ⓔ
❻ *ein(e) Bankangestellte(r)*	**DAS THEATER** ⓕ

Haggle with: 1 d mechanic / garage // 6 e bank clerk / bank
Not haggle with: 2 c baker / bakery // 3 b florist / flower shop // 4 a priest / church // 5 f actor / theatre

4 // After getting all of the necessary repairs done for another great "bargain" (just 127% of the original price!)**, Paul and Linn finally set off. Their eyes lock onto the horizon, their minds dream of the metaphorical landscape of possibilities beyond it, and their hearts swell with the spirit of adventure. Then, about six minutes later, the van breaks down. Put the events from their journey below in order, from first to last.**

	Der Bus fährt schnell.
	Linn sagt: „Ich glaube, wir werden langsamer.“
	Der Bus fährt langsamer als vorher.
	Der Bus wird schneller.
	Linn signalisiert dem Wagen hinter ihr, dass sie dabei ist anzuhalten
2	Der Bus hat sich noch nicht bewegt.
	Linn fährt los.
	Paul sagt: „Ich denke, wir haben angehalten.“
	Der Bus hält an.
1	Paul und Linn sind verwirrt.

Sequence from the top: 5 // 7 // 6 // 4 // 8 // 2 // 3 // 10 // 9 // 1

(1) Paul and Linn are confused. // (2) The van hasn't yet moved. // (3) Linn pulls away. // (4) The van is speeding up. // (5) The van is going fast. // (6) The van is going slower than before. // (7) Linn says, "I think we're slowing down." // (8) Linn signals to the car behind her she is about to stop. // (9) The van stops. // (10) Paul says, "I think we've stopped."

5 // **As usual, the world's kindliest and friendliest people are drawn to Linn and Paul like moths to a flame. Indeed, it's amazing how many people turn up to help, how quickly they turn up, and how much they insist on helping. "Strangers are incredible," Paul thinks, before realising Linn has come to a stop sideways, across three lanes of traffic.**

Look at the inquiries below – which ones don't fit? Track 20

Was ist euer Problem?

Was ist mit deinem Gesicht los?

Braucht ihr Hilfe?

Ist alles in Ordnung?

FRAGEN

Habt ihr eine Panne?

MAGST DU ZAUBERTRICKS?

Entschuldigung … was ist los?

Don't fit: Magst du Zaubertricks? *Do you like magic tricks?* //
Was ist mit deinem Gesicht los? *What's wrong with your face?*
Fit: Was ist euer Problem? *What is your problem?* //
Ist alles in Ordnung? *Is everything OK?* // Entschuldigung … was ist los?
Excuse me … what's going on? // Habt ihr eine Panne? *Have you broken down?* //
Braucht ihr Hilfe? *Do you need any help?*

6 // As firefighters, ambulance crews, police officers, police dogs, helicopter rescue pilots, the coast guard and a bored bystander called Bernd inspect the van for faults, everyone is increasingly perplexed.

At first, it's hard to figure out what's wrong; the engine looks perfect; the wheels are brand new. After checking all of the van's mechanics, what do you think is the most likely problem? Use your knowledge of Paul and Linn to help!

	right	wrong	
❶	☐	☐	Sie haben nicht getankt.
❷	☐	☐	DIE RÄDER SIND ZU QUADRATISCH.
❸	☐	☐	*Die Passagiere sind zu schwer für den Bus.*
❹	☐	☐	*Die Passagiere sind zu cool für den Bus.*
❺	☐	☐	DER BUS HAT SCHLECHTE LAUNE.

Right: (1) *They didn't put any petrol in.*
Wrong: (2) *The wheels are too square.* // (3) *The passengers are too heavy for the van.* // (4) *The passengers are too cool for the van.* // (5) *The van is in a bad mood.*

After putting petrol in their van, Linn and Paul find it 100% more effective as a means of transport. Indeed, they see so many sights that when they arrive at their next destination, they want to give their eyes a rest. Luckily, they stumble across a trendy new "dark" restaurant, where the waiters are blind, and the guests sit in perfect darkness, in order to enhance the taste of the food. It's all very hip.

It's also all very much the kind of place that Paul and Linn should never be allowed in ...

8 Ein Happen im Dunkeln

A Bite in the Dark

1 // After a complicated sequence of clumsiness, Paul and Linn arrive at their table, having only ruined the evenings of about 5 or 6 other guests so far. Not bad for them, in the circumstances.

After the ordeal of seating them, the stressed-out waiter is somewhat relieved to be giving them their food options at last. Without visual cues, however, they understand nothing. Listen to the following conversation. Track 21

What does the waiter mention as one of the options?

1. *Gebratener Lachs mit Kartoffelbrei*
2. *Brot mit Schinken und Käse*
3. *Würstchen mit Tomatensauce*

Right: (1) Gebratener Lachs mit Kartoffelbrei *Pan-fried salmon with mashed potato*

Wrong: (2) Brot mit Schinken und Käse *bread with ham and cheese* // (3) Würstchen mit Tomatensauce *sausages with tomato sauce*

2 // After not understanding the entire menu, Paul and Linn decide to take a "stab in the dark", so to speak. Their food arrives, and they try their best to describe it to each other. It's the perfect opportunity to practise their German.

Can you connect the phrases below to their equivalents?

1	Es riecht wie ...	It tastes like ...	a
2	Es sieht aus wie ...	It sounds like ...	b
3	Es fühlt sich an wie ...	It smells like ...	c
4	Es schmeckt wie ...	It feels like ...	d
5	Es hört sich an wie ...	It looks like ...	e

1c // 2e // 3d // 4a // 5b

3 // After failing to grasp what on earth she could possibly be describing, Linn offers Paul a forkful of her food to try. He quickly realises it is mashed potato on the fork. However, he only realises it is mashed potato, because she has just mashed the mashed potato into his eyes.

(Mashed potato feels famously fluffy on the eyes ...)

Which parts of Paul's face did Linn miss? Label them!

die Wange · die Augenbraue · das Augenlid · die Lippen · das Ohr · die Wimpern

1 ....

2 ....

3 ....

4 ....

5 ....

6 ....

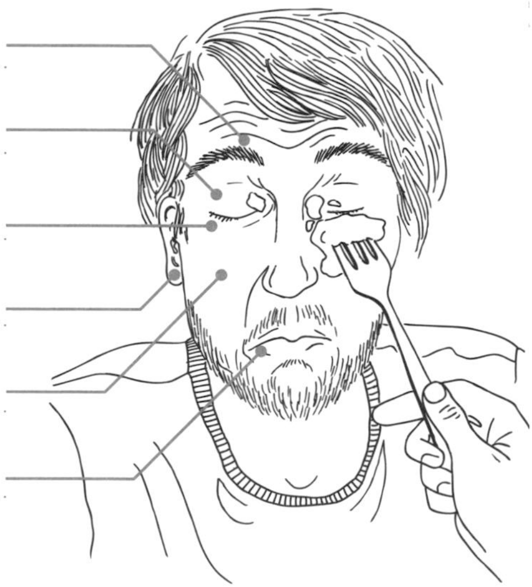

(1) die Augenbraue *eyebrow* // (2) das Augenlid *eyelid* //
(3) die Wimpern *eyelashes* // (4) das Ohr *ear* //
(5) die Wange *cheek* // (6) die Lippen *lips*

4 // Paul decides to go to the "bathroom" to clean up. In a rare moment of foresight, he appreciates in advance the amount that he is probably going to need to apologise in the next few minutes, and decides to practise his German apologies.

Which one is out of place? Track 22

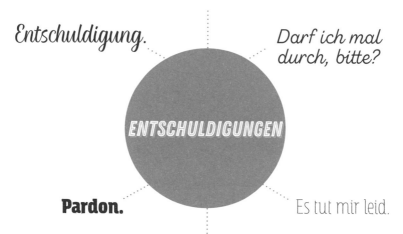

ENTSCHULDIGUNGEN

GUCK DOCH, WO DU HINGEHST!

Entschuldigung.

Darf ich mal durch, bitte?

Pardon.

Es tut mir leid.

Entschuldigen Sie.

Out of place: GUCK DOCH, WO DU HINGEHST!
HEY! WATCH OUT WHERE YOU'RE GOING!

Not out of place: Entschuldigung. *Sorry.* // Entschuldigen Sie. *Excuse me.* // Pardon. *Pardon me.* // Es tut mir leid. *I'm sorry.* // Darf ich mal durch, bitte?
Can I just squeeze past, please?

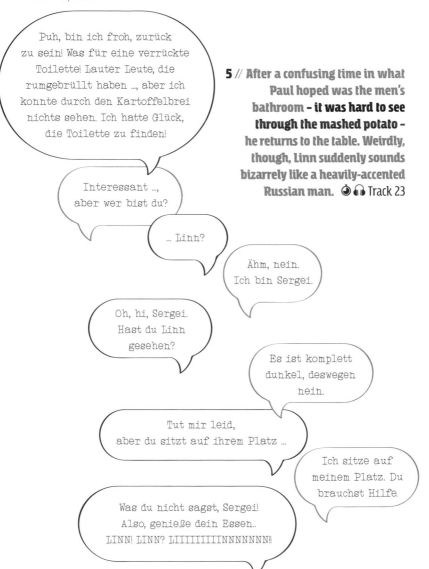

Puh, bin ich froh, zurück zu sein! Was für eine verrückte Toilette! Lauter Leute, die rumgebrüllt haben ..., aber ich konnte durch den Kartoffelbrei nichts sehen. Ich hatte Glück, die Toilette zu finden!

5 // **After a confusing time in what Paul hoped was the men's bathroom – it was hard to see through the mashed potato – he returns to the table. Weirdly, though, Linn suddenly sounds bizarrely like a heavily-accented Russian man.** Track 23

Interessant ..., aber wer bist du?

... Linn?

Ähm, nein. Ich bin Sergei.

Oh, hi, Sergei. Hast du Linn gesehen?

Es ist komplett dunkel, deswegen nein.

Tut mir leid, aber du sitzt auf ihrem Platz ...

Ich sitze auf meinem Platz. Du brauchst Hilfe.

Was du nicht sagst, Sergei! Also, genieße dein Essen.. LINN! LINN? LIIIIIIIIINNNNNNN!!

Phew, I'm glad to be back! What a crazy bathroom! Loads of people were shouting ... but I couldn't see anything through the mash. I was lucky to find the toilet! // Interesting ... but who are you? // ... Linn? // Um, no. I'm Sergei. // Oh, hi, Sergei. Have you seen Linn? // It's 100% dark, therefore no. // Oh, sorry, it's just that you're in her seat ... // I'm in my seat. You need help. // You're telling me, Sergei! Well, enjoy your food ... LINN! LINN? LIIIIIIIIINNNNNNN!!

6 // **Paul and Linn soon find each other again, using only their specially-trained inter-couple powers of echolocation** (him shouting, disturbing everyone, and her turning on her phone torch to find the source of his shouting, disturbing everyone even more).

However, in the loud, sudden light-show, the angry waiter also finds them. Can you figure out why he's so mad? Track 24

die Küche | die ganze Nacht | Gesicht

Kartoffelpüree | zahlt | das Restaurant

Hallo! Bist du der Typ mit (1)..

im (2).. **? Die Köche sagten,**

dass du gerade in (3)..

gekommen bist und in die Spüle gepinkelt hast!

Ich denke, ihr solltet (4)..

verlassen ... und zwar sofort!

Ihr habt (5)..

alle gestört! Bitte (6).................................. **und raus mit euch!**

(1) Kartoffelpüree *mashed potato* // (2) Gesicht *face* // (3) die Küche *kitchen* // (4) das Restaurant *restaurant* // (5) die ganze Nacht *all night* // (6) zahlt *pay*

Hey! Are you the guy with mashed potato on his face? The chefs said that you just came into the kitchen and peed in the sink! I'm afraid you are going to have to leave the restaurant ... right now! You've been disturbing everyone all night! Please pay and get out!

After the clumsy-darkness potato-face torch-shouting incident, Paul and Linn decide to stick with a more traditional (and well-lit) establishment for their next night-time adventure.

Luckily, there's a live band playing at a local bar tonight!
Is it a blues band? A jazz quartet?
A Siberian acapella rock-funk fusion kazoo orchestra?

Who cares! The bar has light-bulbs!

9

Eine wilde Nacht

A Wild Night

1 // As soon as Linn and Paul arrive in what might be the world's best bar, they can instantly feel what a great night it's going to be! Hell, the whole bar looks like an advert for a great bar come to life. There's an Irish band playing, and the whole crowd is drinking, singing, laughing and dancing.

- O Livemusik
- O Tanzen
- O viel Sand
- O eine gute Atmosphäre
- O eine gute Stratosphäre
- O Singen
- O freundliche Menschen
- O Essen und Trinken
- O wütende Echsenbewohner des Planeten Fungobungo

Behind the bar is a checklist on the wall: an apparently fool-proof recipe for fun. Can you guess which items the bar staff have checked off?

Checked off: Livemusik *live music* // Tanzen *dancing* // eine gute Atmosphäre *a good atmosphere* // Singen *singing* // freundliche Menschen *friendly people* // Essen und Trinken *food and drink*

Not checked off: viel Sand *lots of sand* // eine gute Stratosphäre *a good stratosphere* // wütende Echsenbewohner des Planeten Fungobungo *angry lizard people from Planet Fungobungo*

2 // It's not long before Linn and Paul have totally joined the party. Overconfident from the absence of total darkness in the bar, they enthusiastically join in the dance: a high-energy, fast-spinning mass jig. Two tangos and one can-can later, however, they kick each other, breaking one little toe each. Ouch!

They fall down, and the crowd starts shouting seemingly random health advice. Can you separate the advice from the nonsense?

Atme!
Bleib weg vom Licht!
Bleib ruhig!
Versuch draufzuspringen!
Beweg ihn nicht!
Entspann dich!
Wonach riecht er?

Health advice: Beweg ihn nicht! *Don't move it!* // Bleib ruhig! *Keep calm!* // Atme! *Breathe!* // Entspann dich! *Relax!*

Weird advice: Bleib weg vom Licht! *Stay away from the light!* // Versuch draufzuspringen! *Try to jump on it!* // Wonach riecht er? *What does it smell like?*

3 // **Paul and Linn go to hospital by highly unnecessary ambulance, and have to sit in the Accident & Emergency waiting room, feeling quite a lot more Accident than Emergency. Hospitals can be confusing places for anybody, let alone for innately confused tourists like Linn and Paul.**

Can you help them match their fellow patients up with their symptoms below?

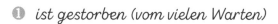

1. *ist gestorben (vom vielen Warten)*
2. *hat zu viel Tequila getrunken*
3. *hat das Innere eines Gefrierschranks für eine Wette abgeleckt*
4. *benutzte eine Tube Kleber als Zahnpasta*
5. *hat versehentlich seinen Penis in seinem Hosenreißverschluss eingeklemmt*
6. *ist traumatisiert (er sah den Penis seines Freundes im Reißverschluss eingeklemmt …)*

a

b

c

d

e

f

1c // 2d // 3f // 4b // 5a // 6e

died (from waiting) // drank too much tequila // licked the inside of a freezer for a bet // used a tube of glue as toothpaste // accidentally caught his penis in his trouser zip // traumatised (he saw his friend's penis get caught in the zip …)

4 // Eventually, a doctor arrives, although, weirdly, he comes in through the front door, then stumbles over a chair, then sings a bit of Lady Gaga, then looks surprised to see all of the patients in the waiting room. After saying hello enthusiastically, hiccuping twice, and then putting his arms around Paul and Linn, he asks them, "What's up?"

Can you help them describe their problem(s)? Add the missing words and find the correct translation.

Schmerz · Zeh · schmerzhaft · Probleme

1. Ich glaube, mein (1) .... ist gebrochen!
2. Der (2) .... kommt und geht.
3. Ich habe (3) ...., meine Flip-Flops anzubehalten.
4. Es ist ziemlich (4) ....!

a. THE PAIN COMES AND GOES.
b. IT'S QUITE PAINFUL
c. I THINK MY TOE IS BROKEN!
d. I'M HAVING A LITTLE TROUBLE KEEPING MY FLIP-FLOPS ON.

Schmerz *pain* // Zeh *toe* // schmerzhaft *painful* // Probleme *trouble*

1c // 2a // 3d // 4b

5 // **The doctor, who upon closer inspection, smells suspiciously like a Tequila Sunrise, leads them into his office, hiccuping loudly, and telling them "not to mind the dog".** (There isn't a dog.)

Once inside the room, the doctor has forgotten who they are, and why they're there. Can you fill in the gaps below? Track 25

wenn er nicht angeschraubt wäre | Gedächtnis

erinnere mich nicht an | passiert | verwirrt

Entschuldigung, ich bin ein bisschen

(1)... .

Was ist noch mal (2).. **? Aha, ja!**

Du hast ein gutes (3).. **!**

Ich nicht! Ich (4)..

.... **alles.**

Ich würde meinen Kopf vergessen,

(5)... .

(1) verwirrt *confused* // (2) passiert *happened* // (3) Gedächtnis *memory* //
(4) erinnere mich nicht an *don't remember* //
(5) wenn er nicht angeschraubt wäre *if it wasn't screwed on*

Sorry, I'm a bit confused. What happened again? Aha, yes!
You have a good memory! I don't! I don't remember everything.
I would forget my head if it wasn't screwed on.

6 // As their doctor begins to search for beer in the medicine cabinet (while singing 'Poker Face'), a second doctor comes into the room. Listen to the conversation. Track 26

David, heute ist dein freier Tag!

Aber diese arme Menschen sind in mein Haus gekommen und brauchen Hilfe!

Aber das ist nicht dein Haus! Wir sind im Krankenhaus!

Warum sollte ich an meinem freien Tag im Krankenhaus sein?! Ich betrinke mich an meinen freien Tagen!

Aber du bist doch betrunken!

Genau! Ich kann also nicht im Krankenhaus sein, oder? Also, wenn es euch nichts ausmacht; heute ist mein freier Tag. Für diese Leute bist du verantwortlich. Jetzt verlasst bitte mein Haus!

David, it's your day off today! // But these poor people came into my house and need help! // But this isn't your house! This is the hospital! // Why would I be at the hospital on my day off?! I get drunk on my days off! // But you are drunk! // Exactly! So I can't be at the hospital, can I? Now, if you don't mind; it's my day off. These people are your responsibility. Now please get out of my house!

Paul and Linn finally return home, safe and sound,
with just a broken bone each and no belongings.

Luckily, they can afford new ones, as they decided to rent out their apartment on Airbnb to some Germans while they were away, and have consequently "earned" a nice chunk of cash in the International Subletting Racket.

As they reach their own front door, however, they hear the ominous, monotonous sounds of minimal techno coming from inside ...

10

Wieder zu Hause

Back Home

1 // Linn and Paul walk into their apartment to find a very awake group of minimal-techno enthusiasts, who seem to have accidentally forgotten to clean up the apartment, or leave the apartment, or sleep.

(It's an easy mistake to make when every song lasts about 12 hours ...)

Their minds suddenly start racing with everything that could have gone wrong or been damaged! Can you find everything?!

Flecken | Rohrbruch | Löcher | Feuer | Schaden

O	J	F	P	P	S	L	E	N	H	K
A	T	Q	M	F	M	X	S	J	T	V
D	R	Z	H	R	X	V	L	J	D	A
S	O	J	Q	H	B	F	B	L	P	I
W	H	P	C	M	B	L	I	Z	Y	B
J	R	L	Ö	C	H	E	R	S	W	N
R	B	E	F	P	F	C	Z	Q	Y	D
R	R	R	M	H	E	K	Z	O	J	L
D	U	S	H	S	U	E	U	U	Ü	D
S	C	H	A	D	E	N	U	T	E	D
L	H	A	Q	D	R	E	W	S	E	M

Down: (der) Rohrbruch *burst pipe(s)* // (das) Feuer *fire* // (die) Flecken *stains*

Across: (die) Löcher *holes* // (der) Schaden *damage*

2 // **They try to get the attention of the very awake-looking "DJ", but unfortunately he seems entirely engrossed in trying to mix one minimal-techno track perfectly into a slightly louder version of itself. Instead, they say hi to another Airbnb guest who is on the couch, wearing one of Linn's sparkliest dresses and staring at his own hands in awed wonder.**

Listen to the conversation. Track 27

WHAT DOES THE AIRBNB GUEST EXPLAIN TO PAUL AND LINN?

a) *Wir sind alle miteinander verbunden.*

b) *Zeit ist eine Illusion.*

c) *Wir sind alle wunderschöne Tiere.*

Right: (b) Zeit ist eine Illusion. *Time is an illusion.*
Wrong: (a) Wir sind alle miteinander verbunden. *We are all connected.* //
(c) Wir sind alle wunderschöne Tiere. *We are all beautiful animals.*

3 // After checking their calendar, Linn and Paul do indeed realise that they are back from their trip one day too early, and therefore cannot get back into their apartment until the concept of "tomorrow" arrives and becomes the concept of "now".

They apologise, and prepare to leave. Can you match up the phrases? Which one is left over?

Bis später! See you soon.

Bis bald! **See you next time.**

Bis morgen! See you later.

Bis nächstes Mal! See you tomorrow.

BIS DANN! SEE YOU THEN.

Bis Weihnachten!

Equivalents: Bis bald! *See you soon.* // Bis nächstes Mal! *See you next time.* // Bis später! *See you later.* // Bis morgen! *See you tomorrow.* // Bis dann! *See you then.*

Left over is: Bis Weihnachten! *See you at Christmas.*

4 // **Seeing how confused, lost and disoriented Paul and Linn now look, the sleep-deprived and highly-mangled Airbnb guests take pity on them, and ask if they'd like to stay.**

They happily agree, and decide to sneakily begin cleaning the apartment and checking in on the jobs they need to do now they're back. Can you put the words in the following phrases in the right order?

❶ auf | Pflanzen | die | Balkon | gießen | dem

....

❷ den / leeren / und / Briefkasten / auswischen

....

❸ sauber | den | machen | Kühlschrank | und | ausräumen

....

❹ **bezahlen | Rechnungen | alle | sofort**

....

❺ **gesamte | staubsaugen | Wohnung | die**

....

(1) die Pflanzen auf dem Balkon gießen *water the plants on the balcony* //
(2) den Briefkasten leeren und auswischen *empty and wipe out the letterbox* //
(3) den Kühlschrank ausräumen und sauber machen *clear out and clean the fridge* //
(4) alle Rechnungen sofort bezahlen *pay all bills immediately* //
(5) die gesamte Wohnung staubsaugen *hoover the entire flat*

5 // **While Paul looks in terror at all of their unpaid bills on the sofa** (while a couple next to him stroke his hair and give him lots of compliments), **Linn suddenly remembers another urgent problem: they've organised a 'Welcome Home, Us!' party in the apartment ... tonight!**

They enlist the most obviously energetic people in the apartment to help. What objects will they need to clean up the mess? Track 28

BESEN

Staubsauger

aufblasbare Puppe

Mariachigruppe

Seife

Wischmopp

Schaufel und Besen

SCHWAMM

Needed: (der) Besen *broom* // (der) Staubsauger *vacuum cleaner* // (der) Wischmopp *mop* // (der) Schwamm *sponge* // (die) Seife *soap* // (die) Schaufel und (der) Besen *dustpan and brush*

Not needed: (die) aufblasbare Puppe *blow-up doll* // (die) Mariachigruppe *Mariachi band*

6 // After taking one disapproving look at the mess, everyone at the party simultaneously thinks, why bother?! After all, there's no better place to throw a party than in a place that is already pre-trashed from a previous party. Everything's ready!

Later, Paul and Linn re-tell some of their most exciting tales to test their newfound German skills. They only need your help with all of the important words! Track 29

versuchten | waren | haben

gelesen hatten | ging | gekauft

❶ Wir .... uns einen VW-Bus .... und sind viel herumgefahren.

❷ Wir haben uns die Zehen gebrochen, als wir .... zu tanzen.

❸ Obwohl wir die Anzeige nicht richtig .... , haben wir den Job in einer Schweine-Käse-Fabrik angenommen.

❹ Wir .... in einem Museum eingeschlossen und der Alarm .... los!

(1) haben / gekauft // (2) versuchten // (3) gelesen hatten // (4) waren / ging

(1) We bought a camper van and travelled around a lot. // (2) We were trying to dance when we broke our toes. // (3) Although we hadn't read the advert properly, we took the job in a pig-cheese factory. // (4) We were locked in a museum and the alarm went off.

Track 30

Hallo und tschüs(s)!	Hello and goodbye!
Hallo!	*Hello!*
Guten Tag!	*Good morning/afternoon!*
Guten Morgen!	*Good morning!*
Guten Abend!	*Good evening!*
Willkommen!	*Welcome!*
Nett, dich kennenzulernen!	*Nice to meet you!*
Nett, Sie kennenzulernen!	*Nice to meet you! (formal)*
Wie geht's?	*How are you?*
Wie geht es Ihnen?	*How are you? (formal)*
Alles gut bei dir?	*Everything okay with you?*
Schön, dich wiederzusehen.	*Nice to see you again.*
Ich muss langsam los.	*I have to get going soon.*
Tschüs(s)!	*Bye!*
Auf Wiedersehen!	*Goodbye!*
Wir sehen uns!	*See you!*
Bis bald!	*See you soon!*
Komm gut nach Hause!	*Safe journey home!*
Gute Reise!	*Have a good trip!*

Track 31

Familie	Family
die Mutter, -̈	*mother*
der Vater, -̈	*father*
das Kind, -er	*child*
die Tochter, -̈	*daughter*
der Sohn, ¨-e	*son*
die Tante, -n	*aunt*
der Onkel, -	*uncle*
die Oma, -s	*gran*
die Großmutter, -̈	*grandmother*
der Opa, -s	*grandpa*
der Großvater, -̈	*grandfather*
die Enkelin, -nen	*granddaughter*
der Enkel, -	*grandson*
der Neffe, -n	*nephew*
die Nichte, -n	*niece*
der Cousin, -s	*cousin*
die Cousine, -n	*cousin*

Track 32

Grundzahlen		Cardinal numbers
1	eins	*one*
2	zwei	*two*
3	drei	*three*
4	vier	*four*
5	fünf	*five*
6	sechs	*six*
7	sieben	*seven*
8	acht	*eight*
9	neun	*nine*
10	zehn	*ten*
11	elf	*eleven*
12	zwölf	*twelve*
13	dreizehn	*thirteen*
14	vierzehn	*fourteen*
15	fünfzehn	*fifteen*
16	sechzehn	*sixteen*
17	siebzehn	*seventeen*
18	achtzehn	*eighteen*
19	neunzehn	*nineteen*
20	zwanzig	*twenty*
30	dreißig	*thirty*

Track 33

Grundzahlen		Cardinal numbers
100	(ein)hundert	*a / one hundred*
101	(ein)hundert(und)eins	*a / one hundred and one*
1.000	(ein)tausend	*a / one thousand*
10.000	zehntausend	*ten thousand*
100.000	(ein)hunderttausend	*a / one hundred thousand*
1.000.000	eine Million	*a / one million*
1.000.000.000	eine Milliarde	*a / one billion*

Track 34

Ordnungszahlen	Ordinal numbers
der / die / das erste	*first*
der / die / das zweite	*second*
der / die / das dritte	*third*
der / die / das vierte	*fourth*
der / die / das fünfte	*fifth*
der / die / das zehnte	*tenth*
der / die / das zwanzigste	*twentieth*
der / die / das dreißigste	*thirtieth*

Track 35

Uhrzeiten	Times of day
der Morgen	*morning*
morgens	*in the morning*
der Mittag	*noon*
mittags	*at noon*
der Abend	*evening*
abends	*in the evening*

13 Uhr	*1pm*	16 Uhr	*4pm*	19 Uhr	*7pm*	22 Uhr	*10pm*
14 Uhr	*2pm*	17 Uhr	*5pm*	20 Uhr	*8pm*	23 Uhr	*11pm*
15 Uhr	*3pm*	18 Uhr	*6pm*	21 Uhr	*9pm*	0/24 Uhr	*12am*

Track 36

Zeitangaben	Expressions of time
vor einem Jahr	*a year ago*
vor zwei Tagen	*two days ago*
vorgestern	*the day before yesterday*
gestern	*yesterday*
heute	*today*
eben gerade	*just now*
jetzt	*now*
gleich	*in a moment*
morgen	*tomorrow*
übermorgen	*the day after tomorrow*
in einer Woche	*in a week*
in einem Monat	*in a month*
in einem Jahr	*in a year*

Track 37

Wochentage	Days of the week
Montag	*Monday*
Dienstag	*Tuesday*
Mittwoch	*Wednesday*
Donnerstag	*Thursday*
Freitag	*Friday*
Samstag	*Saturday*
Sonntag	*Sunday*
das Wochenende	*the weekend*

Track 38

Monate	Months
Januar	*January*
Februar	*February*
März	*March*
April	*April*
Mai	*May*
Juni	*June*
Juli	*July*
August	*August*
September	*September*
Oktober	*October*
November	*November*
Dezember	*December*

Track 39

Nationalitäten	Nationalities
Deutschland	*Germany*
deutsch	*German*
der Deutsche *m* / **die Deutsche** *f*	*German*
Österreich	*Austria*
österreichisch	*Austrian*
der Österreicher *m* / **die Österreicherin** *f*	*Austrian*
die Schweiz	*Switzerland*
schweizerisch	*Swiss*
der Schweizer *m* / **die Schweizerin** *f*	*Swiss*
England	*England*
englisch	*English*
der Engländer *m* / **die Engländerin** *f*	*Englishman / Englishwoman*
der Brite *m* / **die Britin** *f*	*Brit*
Irland	*Ireland*
irisch	*Irish*
der Ire *m* / **die Irin** *f*	*Irishman / Irishwoman*
der Amerikaner *m* / **die Amerikanerin** *f*	*American*
der Kanadier *m* / **die Kanadierin** *f*	*Canadian*
der Australier *m* / **die Australierin** *f*	*Australian*
der Neuseeländer *m* / **die Neuseeländerin** *f*	*New Zealander*

Track 40

Orientierung	Orientation
geradeaus	*straight ahead*
rechts	*right*
links	*left*
die Richtung, -en	*direction*
rückwärts	*backwards*
vorwärts	*forwards*
umkehren	*to turn around*
hinter	*behind*
vor	*in front of*
über	*over*
unter	*under*
neben	*next to*
gegenüber	*opposite*

Track 41

Verkehrsmittel	Means of transport
das Auto, -s	*car*
der VW-Bus, -se	*VW camper van*
die U-Bahn, -en	*underground*
das Motorrad, ¨-er	*motorcycle*
das Fahrrad, ¨-er	*bicycle*
das Dreirad, ¨-er	*tricycle*
das Tandem, -s	*tandem*
das Flugzeug, -e	*aeroplane*
das Einrad, ¨-er	*unicycle*
der LKW, -s	*lorry*

Track 42

Wetter	Weather
der Regen	*rain*
Es regnet.	*It's raining.*
der Nieselregen	*drizzle*
Es nieselt.	*It's drizzling.*
Es schüttet.	*It's pouring down.*
die Wolke, -n	*cloud*
die Temperatur, -en	*temperature*
die Sonne, -n	*sun*
Die Sonne scheint.	*The sun is shining.*
der Wind, -e	*wind*
Es ist so windig.	*It is so windy.*
der Sturm, ¨-e	*storm*
Es stürmt.	*It's blowing a gale.*
der Hagel	*hail*
Es hagelt.	*It's hailing.*
der Schnee	*snow*
Es schneit.	*It's snowing.*
Es ist so kalt draußen.	*It is so cold outside.*
Es ist so heiß.	*It is so hot.*

Track 43

Farben	Colours
rot	*red*
rosa	*pink*
orange	*orange*
gelb	*yellow*
grün	*green*
dunkelgrün	*dark green*
blau	*blue*
hellblau	*light/pale blue*
lila	*purple*
violett	*violet*
braun	*brown*
schwarz	*black*
weiß	*white*

einfarbig	*monochrome*
bunt, farbenfroh	*colourful*
grell	*flashy/garish*
hell	*light*
dunkel	*dark*

Track 44

Getränke	Drinks
das Wasser, -	*water*
der Saft, ⸚e	*juice*
der Kaffee, -s	*coffee*
die Cola, -s	*coke*
die Schorle, -n	*spritzer*
der Tee, -s	*tea*
die heiße Schokolade, -n	*hot chocolate*
das Bier, -e	*beer*
der Wein, -e	*wine*
der Schnaps, ⸚e	*schnapps*
der Cocktail, -s	*cocktail*
der Longdrink, -s	*long drink*

Track 45

Einkaufen (Geschäfte)	Shopping (Shops)
der Supermarkt, ⸚e	*supermarket*
die Drogerie, -n	*chemist's*
die Reinigung, -en	*dry cleaner's*
das Blumengeschäft, -e	*flower shop*
die Bäckerei, -en	*bakery*
die Metzgerei, -en	*butcher's*
die Apotheke, -n	*pharmacy*
das Einkaufszentrum, -tren	*shopping centre*
der Wochenmarkt, ⸚e	*weekly market*
das Kaufhaus, Kaufhäuser	*department store*

Track 46

Obst und Gemüse	Fruit and vegetables
das Obst	*fruit*
die Banane, -n	*banana*
der Apfel, ¨-	*apple*
die Kiwi, -s	*kiwi*
die Birne, -n	*pear*
die Pflaume, -n	*plum*
die Kirsche, -n	*cherry*
die Ananas, -	*pineapple*
das Gemüse	*vegetables*
die Karotte, -n	*carrot*
die Tomate, -n	*tomato*
die Paprika, -s	*pepper*
der Sellerie, -	*celery*
der Pilz, -e	*mushroom*
der Brokkoli, -	*broccoli*

Track 47

Linns und Pauls Hobbys	Linn's and Paul's hobbies
reisen	*travelling*
schlafen	*sleeping*
ein Nickerchen machen	*napping*
Bücher lesen	*reading books*
Tischtennis spielen	*playing table tennis*
Trompete spielen	*playing the trumpet*
kochen	*cooking*
tauchen	*scuba diving*
ins Kino gehen	*going to the cinema*
Tandem fahren	*riding a tandem*
ins Museum gehen	*going to museums*
Musik hören	*listening to music*
Bier trinken	*drinking beer*
mit Freunden rumhängen	*hanging out with friends*
Abenteuer erleben	*having adventures*
Essen gehen	*eating out*
feiern gehen	*partying*
fotografieren	*taking photos*

Track 48

Krass! Ausdrücke des Erstaunens	Wow! Expressions of astonishment
Großartig!	*Great!*
Super!	*Super!*
Oh wie schön!	*Oh how lovely!*
Wunderbar!	*Wonderful!*
Toll!	*Awesome!*
Perfekt!	*Perfect!*
Unglaublich!	*Incredible!*
Das ist ja irre!	*That's crazy!*
Krass!	*Wow!*
Oh mein Gott!	*Oh my god!*
Ach!	*Oh! / Ah! / Alas!*
Das kann doch nicht wahr sein!	*That can't be true!*
Wie schrecklich!	*How horrible!*
Wie furchtbar!	*How terrible!*
Scheiße!/Kacke!	*Shit!*
Verdammt!	*Damn!*
Verdammte Scheiße!	*Bloody hell!*
Wie dumm ist das denn?!	*How stupid is that?!*

Track 49

Ich packe meinen Koffer	I pack my suitcase
der Reisepass, ¨-e	*passport*
das Portemonnaie, -s	*wallet*
der Schlüssel, -	*key*
der Kopfhörer, -	*headphones*
die Kulturtasche, -n	*toiletry bag*
die Sonnencreme, -s	*sun cream*
das Aufladekabel, -	*charging cable*
die Brille, -n	*glasses*
der Rasierer, -	*shaver*
die Zahnbürste, -n	*toothbrush*
das Deo, -s	*deodorant*
der Lippenstift, -e	*lipstick*
die Wimperntusche, -n	*mascara*
das Rouge, -	*blusher*
der Lidschatten, -	*eyeshadow*
der Kajalstift, -e	*eyeliner*
das Parfum, -s	*perfume*
das Shampoo, -s	*shampoo*
die Seife, -n	*soap*
der Tampon, -s	*tampon*
das Kondom, -e	*condom*
die Kopfschmerztablette, -n	*headache tablet*
das Handy, -s	*mobile phone*
das Handtuch, ¨-er	*towel*
die Haarbürste, -n	*hair brush*

Track 49

Ich packe meinen Koffer	I pack my suitcase
die Hose, -n	*trousers*
das Hemd, -en	*shirt*
das T-Shirt, -s	*T-shirt*
das Kleid, -er	*dress*
die Unterwäsche, -	*underwear*
der BH, -s	*bra*
die Unterhose, -n	*underpants*
die Socke, -n	*sock*
der Schuh, -e	*shoe*
die Jacke, -n	*jacket*
der Mantel, ¨-	*coat*
die Strumpfhose, -n	*tights*
der Badeanzug, ¨-e	*swimming costume*
die Badehose, -n	*swimming trunks*
der Rucksack, ¨-e	*backpack*
die Handtasche, -n	*handbag*
die Armbanduhr, -en	*wristwatch*
die Kette, -n	*necklace*
der Ring, -e	*ring*
der Armreif, -e	*bracelet*
der Ohrring, -e	*earring*

Track 50

Körperteile	Parts of the body
der Kopf, ¨-e	*head*
die Schulter, -n	*shoulder*
das Gesicht, -er	*face*
die Stirn, -en	*forehead*
die Nase, -n	*nose*
der Mund, ¨-er	*mouth*
das Ohr, -en	*ear*
die Backe, -n	*cheek*
das Haar, -e	*hair*
das Kinn, -e	*chin*
der Arm, -e	*arm*
die Hand, ¨-e	*hand*
der Finger, -	*finger*
der Bauch, ¨-e	*belly*
die Hüfte, -n	*hip*
der Po, -s	*bottom / bum*
das Bein, -e	*leg*
das Knie, -	*knee*
der Fuß, ¨-e	*foot*
der Zeh, -en	*toe*
der Magen, ¨-en	*stomach*

Track 51

Möbel	Furniture
der Stuhl, ¨-e	*chair*
das Sofa, -s	*sofa*
der Tisch, -e	*table*
der Schreibtisch, -e	*desk*
der Esstisch, -e	*dining table*
der Sessel, -	*armchair*
der Schrank, ¨-e	*wardrobe*
die Kommode, -n	*chest of drawers*
der Nachttisch, -e	*bedside table*
das Bett, -en	*bed*
das Doppelbett, -en	*double bed*
die Lampe, -n	*lamp*
das Regal, -e	*bookshelves*
der Hocker, -	*stool*
die Bank, ¨-e	*bench*
die Garderobe, -n	*coatrack*
der Kühlschrank, ¨-e	*fridge*
der Spiegel, -	*mirror*
der Teppich, -e	*rug/carpet*
der Liegestuhl, ¨-e	*deck chair*

Personal pronouns

ich	*I*
du	*you Sg inform*
er / sie / es	*he / she / it*
wir	*we*
ihr	*you Pl inform*
sie	*they*
Sie	*you Sg / Pl form*

Regular verbs

Regular verbs in the present tense in German are formed from the stem (e.g. **mach-**) of the infinitive (e.g. **machen**), plus the following endings:

machen *to make / to do*	gehen *to go*
ich mach**e**	ich geh**e**
du mach**st**	du geh**st**
er / sie / es mach**t**	er / sie / es geh**t**
wir mach**en**	wir geh**en**
ihr mach**t**	ihr geh**t**
sie mach**en**	sie geh**en**
Sie mach**en**	Sie geh**en**

Irregular verbs

Not all German verbs are regular, however, and many of the most important ones are irregular:

sein *to be*	haben *to have*
ich bin	ich habe
du bist	du hast
er / sie / es ist	er / sie / es hat
wir sind	wir haben
ihr seid	ihr habt
sie sind	sie haben
Sie sind	Sie haben

Linn und Paul **sind** ein chaotisches Pärchen.
Linn and Paul are a chaotic couple.

Sie **haben** kein Geld. *They have no money.*

werden *going to*
ich werde
du wirst
er / sie / es wird
wir werden
ihr werdet
sie werden
Sie werden

Modal auxiliary verbs

Here are the modal verbs and how to conjugate them:

können *can*	müssen *must**	wollen *to want*
ich kann	ich muss	ich will
du kannst	du musst	du willst
er / sie / es kann	er / sie / es muss	er / sie / es will
wir können	wir müssen	wir wollen
ihr könnt	ihr müsst	ihr wollt
sie können	sie müssen	sie wollen
Sie können	Sie müssen	Sie wollen

dürfen *to be allowed to*	sollen *to be supposed to*	mögen *to like*
ich darf	ich soll	ich mag
du darfst	du sollst	du magst
er / sie / es darf	er / sie / es soll	er / sie / es mag
wir dürfen	wir sollen	wir mögen
ihr dürft	ihr sollt	ihr mögt
sie dürfen	sie sollen	sie mögen
Sie dürfen	Sie sollen	Sie mögen

*Be careful! *You must not* ... is „Du darfst nicht ..." **not** „Du musst nicht ...!"

Articles

Nouns in German can be masculine, feminine or neuter, so there are three possible definite articles for indicating a noun's gender (Genus) in the nominative singular case. There is also a fourth article, **die**, for plurals of any gender. Indefinite articles in German can be either **ein** *m/n* or **eine** *f*:

The definite article *(the)*	The indefinite article *(a, an)*
der *m*	**ein** *m*
die *f*	**eine** *f*
das *n*	**ein** *n*
die *Pl*	--

der Rock *m* *the skirt*

die Reise *f* *the trip*

das Pärchen *n* *the couple*

die Autos *Pl* *the cars*

ein Baum *m* *a tree*

eine Zwiebel *f* *an onion*

As you can see, there is not much logic to genders (with a few exceptions) like **der Mann** or **die Frau**.

Adjectives

Following the indefinite article, adjectives take endings which reflect the gender of the noun they are attached to.
The table shows examples in the nominative case.

	Definite article	Indefinite article
m	der schön**e** Bus *the beautiful bus*	ein schön**er** Bus *a beautiful bus*
f	die schön**e** Reise *the beautiful trip*	eine schön**e** Reise *a beautiful trip*
n	das schön**e** Pärchen *the beautiful couple*	ein schön**es** Pärchen *a beautiful couple*
Pl	die schön**en** Pantoffeln *the beautiful slippers*	meine schön**en** Pantoffeln *my beautiful slippers*

Negations

Nicht negates a sentence or part of a sentence:

Ich sehe was, was du **nicht** siehst, und das ist blau.
I see something that you can't see and it's blue.

Kein is used when **nicht** would otherwise be followed by an indefinite article, i.e. **nicht + ein = kein; nicht + eine = keine**:

Das ist **kein** Flugzeug! *That's not an aeroplane!*

Das ist **keine** Vase! *That's not a vase!*

Das ist **kein** Hund! *That's not a dog!*

Present and perfect tense

The simple present tense is the most commonly used temporal form in German. It is used to convey both the simple and continuous present tenses in English:

Linn und Paul **fahren** zum Flughafen.
Linn and Paul drive to the airport.
Linn and Paul are driving to the airport.

The perfect tense describes an already completed action. The verbs are combined with the present tense of either **sein** *to be* or **haben** *to have* – depending on whether the verb describes motion or not – and the past participle of the verb:

Linn und Paul **sind** zu schnell **losgefahren**.
Linn and Paul drove off too quickly.

Paul **hat** seinen Pass **vergessen**.
Paul has forgotten his passport.

Imperatives

The imperative is used to give instructions or make requests or suggestions:

	warten *to wait*	singen *to sing*
Sg inform	Wart**e**!	Sing(**e**)!
Pl inform	Wart**et**!	Sing**t**!
Sg/Pl form	Wart**en Sie**!	Sing**en Sie**!

Sing bitte für mich! *Please sing for me!*

Wartet auf mich! *Wait for me!*

Essen Sie die Wurst! *Eat the sausage!*

Possessive pronouns

Possessive pronouns indicate possession (surprisingly!). In German, they also reflect the gender of the noun they qualify. The following table gives you the possessive pronouns in the nominative case:

sein Hund *m* *his dog*

mein**e** Katze *f* *my cat*

dein Pferd *n* *your horse*

mein / e	*my*
dein / e	*your Sg inform*
sein / e	*his*
ihr / e	*her*
sein / e	*its*
unser / uns(e)re	*our*
euer / eure	*your Pl inform*
ihr / e	*their*
Ihr / e	*your Sg/Pl form*

Meine Familie bringt uns zum Flughafen.
My family is taking us to the airport.

Hier ist **dein** Wechselgeld. *Here is your change.*

Asking questions + question words

In German, questions are formed by the inversion of the pronoun (e.g. **er**) and the verb (e.g. **hat**) in a sentence:

Er hat einen Job. **Hat er** einen Job?

Questions in English are often formed with the verb *to do* but there is no equivalent of this in German:

*Does **he have** a job?* **Hat er** einen Job?

Question words

Wer?	*Who?*
Was?	*What?*
Wo?	*Where?*
Welche(r/s)?	*Which (one)?*
Warum?	*Why?*
Wie?	*How?*
Wozu?	*What ... for?*
Wessen?	*Whose?*
Woher?	*From where?/Where ... from?*

Questions with question words begin with the question word:

Warum sollte ich an meinem freien Tag im Krankenhaus sein?!
Why should I be in the hospital on my day off?!

Prepositions come at the beginning of the sentence:

Mit wem verreist du? *Who are you travelling with?*

Für wen sind die Blumen? *Who are the flowers for?*

Kapitel 2.1 **Lost in the Mall** Track 8

Jakob:	Hallo.	Jakob:	*Hello.*
Paul:	Äh ... Hallo.	Paul:	*Er... hello.*
Jakob:	Habt ihr Geld?	Jakob:	*Have you got any money?*
Paul:	Ja, auf jeden Fall! Machen Sie sich keine Sorgen, wir haben viel Geld und werden auf jeden Fall etwas kaufen. Wir sind im Urlaub und haben all unsere Sachen verloren.	Paul:	*Yes, of course! Don't worry, we've got lots of money and are definitely going to buy something. We are on holiday and have lost everything.*
Jakob:	Oh nein, das tut mir leid. Aber hast du etwas Kleingeld?	Jakob:	*Oh no, I'm sorry. But have you got any change?*
Linn:	Nein, wir haben nur großes Geld. Wir haben aber genug Geld für alles, was wir kaufen wollen, ganz sicher! Wir haben alles verloren!	Linn:	*No, we don't have any change. But we've definitely got enough money to buy everything we need. We've lost everything!*
Jakob:	Okay, wow, das ist alles wirklich interessant. Aber habt ihr etwas Kleingeld ... für mich?	Jakob:	*Ok, wow, that's all really interesting, but do you have any change ... for me?*

Kapitel 3.1 **Bored with a Stranger** Track 10

Linn:	Und was machst du so?	Linn:	*And what do you do?*
Luzie:	Buchhaltung. Ich arbeite in der Buchhaltung einer Buchhaltungsfirma. Wir kümmern uns um die Buchhaltung anderer Buchhaltungsgesellschaften.	Luzie:	*Accounts. I work in the accounting department of an accounting company. We do the accounts for other accounting companies.*
Paul:	Wow, das ist ... ähm ... wirklich cool. Und hast du ...irgendwelche Hobbys?	Paul:	*Wow, that's ... um ... really cool. And do you have ... any hobbies?*
Luzie:	Ich mag Buchhaltung. Ist das ein Hobby? Ich mag auch Brot. Aber nicht, um es zu essen. Eigentlich mag ich kein Brot. Ich bevorzuge Tabellen.	Luzie:	*I like doing accounting. Is that a hobby? I also like bread. Not eating it, though. Actually, I don't like bread. I prefer accounts.*
Linn:	Und ... ähm ... hm ... wie lange arbeitest du schon in der ... äh ... Buchhaltung?	Linn:	*And ... er ... um ... how long have you ... er ... been doing accounting for?*
Luzie:	Großartige Frage! Ich gehe meinen Taschenrechner holen. Das wird ein Spaß.	Luzie:	*Great question! I'll go and get my calculator. This will be fun.*

Kapitel 4.1 **An Increasingly Tricky Pub Visit** Track 12

Typ 1:	Dieses Mal ist es meine Runde!	Guy 1:	*It's my round this time!*
Typ 2:	Nein, nein, nein! Letztes Mal war es deine Runde... jetzt bin ich dran! Ich bestehe darauf!	Guy 2:	*No, no, no! It was your round last time ... now it's my turn! I insist!*

Typ 3:	Danke, Leute, aber leider liegt ihr beide falsch. Ihr habt schon Runden bezahlt. Das ist jetzt meine Runde.	Guy 3:	*Thanks, guys, but unfortunately you are both wrong. You already bought rounds. It is my round now.*
Typ 4:	Quatsch! Es ist ganz, ganz, ganz eindeutig meine Runde! Ich bin mir fast sicher. Entschuldigung, Barkeeper ... sechs Bier bitte!	Guy 4:	*Nonsense! It is definitely, definitely, definitely my round! I'm almost positive. Excuse me, bartender ... Six beers, please!*

Kapitel 5.5 Scared in the Museum Track 15

Stefan:	Ich habe gruselige leuchtende Gesichter gesehen und seltsame Geistergeschichten gehört, die aus der Dunkelheit kamen, also habe ich mich versteckt. Ich verstecke mich immer.	Stefan:	*I just saw scary glowing faces and heard strange ghost stories coming out of the darkness, so I hid. I always hide.*
Paul:	Es tut uns sehr leid!	Paul:	*We are so sorry!*
Linn:	Wir sind keine Geister, wir sind nur verwirrt!	Linn:	*We are not ghosts, we are just confused!*
Stefan:	Ich bin so froh, dass ihr nur normale Menschen seid, die eingeschlossen wurden.	Stefan:	*I'm so glad you're just some normal humans that got locked in.*
Linn:	Ja, wir sind nur normale Menschen, die eingeschlossen wurden.	Linn:	*Yep, we're just normal humans that got locked in.*
Paul:	Ich wette, es passiert dauernd, dass Leute eingeschlossen werden, oder?	Paul:	*I bet peoplea get locked in all the time, huh?*
Stefan:	Ähm, nein. Meistens sind es nur Geister.	Stefan:	*Um, no. Mostly it's just ghosts.*

Kapitel 7.1 A Breakdown Track 19

Verkäufer:	2.000.	Seller:	*2000.*
Paul:	2.999?	Paul:	*2999?*
Verkäufer:	Äh, okay ... dann 3.000?	Seller:	*Er, ok ... 3000, then?*
Paul:	17.968!	Paul:	*17,968!*
Verkäufer:	Oh, äh ... wow. Äh ... nein, soviel kann ich nicht annehmen.	Seller:	*Oh, er ... wow. Er ... no, I couldn't take that much.*
Paul:	6!	Paul:	*6!*
Verkäufer:	Nein.	Seller:	*No.*
Paul:	Wie wäre es mit 3.500?	Paul:	*How about 3500?*
Verkäufer:	Ähm, okay. Also. Sagen wir 3.501. Abgemacht?	Seller:	*Um, ok. Right. Let's say 3501. Deal?*
Paul:	Abgemacht!	Paul:	*Deal!*

Kapitel 8.1 A Bite in the Dark Track 21

Gestresster Kellner:	Mein Gott, das war stressig! Ich glaube, Sie haben wirklich jeden einzelnen Tisch angerempelt!	**Stressed Waiter:**	*My god, that was stressful! I think you hit every table!*
Paul:	Entschuldigung, es schien mir einfach sicherer, zu laufen anstatt zu gehen.	**Paul:**	*Sorry, it just seemed safer to run.*
Gestresster Kellner:	Was ?! Warum?! Das ist gefährlich!	**Stressed Waiter:**	*What?! Why?! It's dangerous!*
Linn:	Genau! Wir wollten schneller an unseren Tisch kommen!	**Linn:**	*Exactly! We wanted to get to our table quicker!*
Gestresster Kellner:	Was?! Okay, vergessen Sie es. Bitte setzen Sie sich jetzt. Jetzt. Bitte!	**Stressed Waiter:**	*What?! OK, never mind. Just please sit down. Now. Please!*
Paul & Linn (zusammen):	Danke! Vielen Dank!	**Paul & Linn (together):**	*Thanks! Thank you!*
Gestresster Kellner:	Sie sitzen auf dem Tisch. Bitte setzen Sie sich auf die Stühle.	**Stressed Waiter:**	*You're sitting on the table. Please sit on the chairs.*
Paul & Linn (zusammen):	Ups, Entschuldigung! Ah ja, das ist eine viel bessere Idee.	**Paul & Linn (together):**	*Oops, sorry! Ah, that's a much better idea.*
Gestresster Kellner:	Oh Gott ... okay ... heute Abend gibt es drei Optionen: ein Knoblauch-Pilz-Risotto, gebratener Lachs mit Kartoffelbrei oder Spaghetti Bolognaise. Ich bitte Sie, sich schnell zu entscheiden! Sie machen mich fertig!	**Stressed Waiter:**	*My god... ok... tonight there's three options: a garlic mushroom risotto, pan-fried salmon with mashed potato, or spaghetti bolognaise. Please choose quickly! You're stressing me out!*

Kapitel 10.2 Back Home Track 27

Airbnb Gast:	Whoah, hey! Guten Abend!	**Airbnb guest:**	*Whoah, hey! Good evening!*
Paul:	Es ist schon Morgen.	**Paul:**	*It's morning.*
Airbnb Gast:	Genau, Mann! Zeit ist eine Illusion! Morgen? Abend? Das sind doch nur Konzepte ... ne?	**Airbnb guest:**	*Exactly, man! Time is an illusion! Morning? Evening? They're just, like, concepts ... right?*
Linn:	Ähm, ich habe noch nie darüber nachgedacht, aber ich denke, du hast recht! Ähm, entschuldige, aber ich glaube, dass ihr heute Morgen unsere Wohnung verlassen solltet. Wir sind zurück von unserer Reise!	**Linn:**	*Um, I never thought about it, but I suppose that's true! Um, sorry, but I think that you were supposed to leave our apartment this morning. We're back from our trip!*
Airbnb Gast:	Whoah, das ist so cool, Mann. Es ist nur so, dass wir erst morgen früh hier raus müssen. Die Zeit ist also doch keine Illusion. Guck mal in deinen Kalender.	**Airbnb guest:**	*Whoah, that's, like, so cool, man. It's just that we're supposed to leave tomorrow morning. Time's not that much of an illusion, you know. Check your calendar.*

A

Abend, -e *m evening*
abends *in the evening*
Abenteuer erleben *to have adventures*
aber *but, however, though*
abgemacht *deal*
ablenken *to distract*
abschicken *to send*
Ach! *Oh!, Ah!, Alas!*
acht *eight*
achtzehn *eighteen*
Adresse, -n *f address*
aha *aha*
alle *everybody, everyone, all*
allein *alone*
allergisch *allergic*
alles *everything*
Alpen *Pl Alps*
als *as; than; when*
also *so; well*
am *against the; on the; at the*
Amerikaner *m /* **Amerikanerin** *f American*
an *against; on; at*
Ananas, - *f pineapple*
anbehalten *to keep on*
andere(r, -s) *other*
angenommen *assumed, assuming*
anhalten *to stop*
annehmen *to suppose; to accept*
anschrauben *to screw on*
anschreiben *to write to*
anzeigen *to show*
anziehen; sich **anziehen** *to put on; to dress*
Apfel, ̈- *m apple*
Apotheke, -n *f pharmacy*
April *April*
Arbeit, -en *f job; work*
arm *poor*
Arm, -e *m arm*
Armbanduhr, -en *f wristwatch*
Armreif, -e *m bracelet*
atmen *to breathe*
Atmosphäre, -n *f atmosphere*
auch *also, too*
auf *at; on*
Auf Wiedersehen! *Goodbye!*
Aufladekabel, - *n charging cable*
aufladen *to charge*
aufstehen *to get up*
Augenbraue, -n *f eyebrow*
Augenlid, -er *n eyelid*
August *August*
aus *from*
Ausdruck, ̈-e *m expression*
ausdrücken *to express; to squeeze*
Ausgang, ̈-e *m exit*
ausleihen *to lend*
ausmachen *to put out*
Auspuff, -e *m exhaust*
ausräumen *to clear out*
außerirdisch *extraterrestrial*
Australier *m /* **Australierin** *f Australian*
auswischen *to wipe out*
Auto, -s *n car*
Autowerkstatt, ̈-en *f garage, car repair shop*

B

Backe, -n *f cheek*
Bäcker *m /* **Bäckerin** *f baker*
Bäckerei, -en *f bakery*
Badeanzug, ̈-e *m swimming costume*
Badehose, -n *f swimming trunks*
Badezimmer, - *n bathroom*
bald *soon*
Balkon, -e *m balcony*
Banane, -n *f banana*
Banjo, -s *n banjo*
Bank, -en *f bank*
Bank, ̈-e *f bench*
Bankverbindung, -en *f bank details*
Barkeeper, - *m barman*
Batterie, -n *f battery*
Bauch, ̈-e *m belly*
Bauchschmerzen *Pl stomachache*
Beförderung, -en *f promotion*
bei *with; at*
Bein, -e *n leg*
bekommen *to get*
Bemerkung, -en *f remark*
benutzen *to use*
Benzin *n petrol*
beschwipst *tipsy*

Besen, - *m* *broom*
besoffen *smashed*
besonders *especially*
Besuch, -e *m* *visit*
betrunken *drunk*
Bett, -en *n* *bed*
betteln *to beg*
bevor *before*
sich **bewegen** *to move*
sich **bewerben** *to apply*
Bewerbung, -en *f* *application*
bewusstlos *unconscious*
bezahlen *to pay for*
BH, -s *m* *bra*
Bier, -e *n* *beer*
Bier trinken *to drink beer*
Birne, -n *f* *pear*
bis *till, until*
Bis bald! *See you soon!*
Bis dann! *See you!*
Bis morgen! *Till tomorrow!*
Bis später! *See you later!*
bitte *please; you're welcome*
bitten *to ask*
blau *blue*
Blumenladen, ¨-en *m* *florist's*
blutig *bloody*
borgen *to borrow*
brauchen *to need*
braun *brown*
brechen *to break*
Briefkasten, ¨-en *m* *letterbox; postbox*
Brille, -n *f* *glasses*
Brite *m* / **Britin** *f* *Brit*
Brokkoli, - *m* *broccoli*
Brot, -e *n* *bread*
Brust, ¨-e *f* *breast, chest*
Bücher lesen *to read books*
bunt *colourful*
Bus, -se *m* *bus*

C

Cent, -s *m* *cent*
chillen *to chill (out)*
Christus *m* *Christ*
Cocktail, -s *m* *cocktail*
Cola, -s *f* *coke*
cool *cool*
Cousin, -s *m* *cousin*
Cousine, -n *f* *cousin*

D

da *there*
dabei *present*
danke *thank you*
dann *then*
daran *on it; that*
dass *that*
denken *to think*
denn *because*
Deo, -s *n* *deodorant*
deutsch *German*
Deutsche *m* / **Deutsche** *f* *German*
Deutschland *Germany*
Dezember *December*
Dienstag *Tuesday*
diese(r, -s) *this*
doch *yes; however*
Donnerstag *Thursday*
Doppelbett, -en *n* *double bed*
draußen *outside*
drehen *to turn*
drei *three*
Dreirad, ¨-er *n* *tricycle*
dreißig *thirty*
dreizehn *thirteen*
Drogerie, -n *f* *chemist's*
drucken *to print*
Du bist dran. *It's your turn.*
dumm *stupid*
dunkel *dark*
Dunkelheit, - *f* *darkness*
dunkelgrün *dark green*
durch *through; by*
dürfen *may, to be allowed to, can*
durstig *thirsty*
Dusche, -n *f* *shower*
duschen *to have a shower*
Duschgel, -e *n* *shower gel*

E

eben gerade *just now*
eh *hey*
ein(e) *a, an; one*

ein bisschen *a bit, a little*
einfarbig *monochrome*
Eingang, ¨-e *m* *entrance*
eingeklemmt *stuck*
(ein)hundert *a/one hundred*
(ein)hundert(und)eins *a/one hundred and one*
(ein)hunderttausend *a/one hundred thousand*
einkaufen *to buy; to shop*
Einkaufszentrum, -tren *n* *shopping centre*
Einrad, ¨-er *n* *unicycle*
eins *one*
einschlafen *to fall asleep, to go to sleep*
einschließen *to lock up*
(ein)tausend *a/one thousand*
Eis, - *n* *ice; ice cream*
Elektrizität *f* *electricity*
elf *eleven*
Ende, -n *n* *end, finish*
England *England*
Engländer *m* / **Engländerin** *f* *Englishman / Englishwoman*
englisch *English*
Enkel, - *m* *grandson*
Enkelin, -nen *f* *granddaughter*
entschuldigen *to excuse*
Entschuldigung, -en *f* *apology*
Entschuldigung! *Excuse me!, Sorry!, Pardon!*
erhalten *to receive*
Erkältung, -en *f* *cold*
jmdn. **erstaunen** *to astonish s.o.*
Es tut mir leid. *I'm sorry.*
essen *to eat*
essen gehen *to eat out*
Esstisch, -e *m* *dining table*
etwas *something, anything; some, any*

F

fahren *to drive, to go*
Fahrrad, ¨-er *n* *bicycle*
Familie, -n *f* *family*
Farbe, -n *f* *colour*
farbenfroh *colourful*
fast *nearly, almost*
Favorit, -en *m* *favourite*
Februar *February*
feiern gehen *to party*
Fernsehen *n* *television, TV*
Fernseher, - *m* *TV*
Festival, -s *n* *festival*
Feuer, - *n* *fire*
Feuerwehrleute *Pl* *firefighters*
filmen *to film*
Finanzsektor, -en *m* *financial sector*
finden *to find*
Finger, - *m* *finger*
Fleck, -en *m* *stain*
Flug, ¨-e *m* *flight*
Flughafen, ¨ *m* *airport*
Flugzeug, -e *n* *aeroplane*
Foto, -s *n* *photo*
fotografieren *to take photos*
frei *free*
Freitag *Friday*
Freizeit, -en *f* *free time*
fremd *foreign*
sich **freuen** *to be glad*
Freund *m* / **Freundin** *f* *friend*
freundlich *friendly, kind*
froh *glad*
früh *early*
sich **fühlen** *to feel*
fünf *five*
fünfzehn *fifteen*
für *for*
furchtbar *terrible*
sich **fürchten** *to be afraid*
Fuß, ¨-e *m* *foot*

G

ganz *completely*
Garderobe, -n *f* *coatrack*
geben *to give*
gebrochen *broken*
Gedächtnis *n* *memory*
gegen *against*
gegenüber *opposite*
Geheimnummer, -n *f* *PIN number*
gehen *to go, to walk*
gekauft *bought*
gekocht *cooked*
gelangweilt *bored*
gelb *yellow*

Geld, -er *n money*
Gemüse *n vegetables*
genau *exact; exactly*
genießen *to enjoy*
genug *enough*
gerade *straight; just*
geradeaus *straight ahead*
geradezu *virtually*
Geräusch, -e *n sound*
gern *willingly*
gesamt *whole, entire*
Geschäft, -e *n shop*
Geschenk, -e *n present*
geschickt *skilful*
Geschwister *Pl brothers and sisters, siblings*
Gesicht, -er *n face*
gestern *yesterday*
gestorben *died*
gestört *disturbed*
Getränk, -e *n drink*
gießen *to water*
Gift, -e *n poison*
Gin, -s *m gin*
glauben *to believe, to think*
gleich *in a moment*
Glück *n luck*
Gott, ¨-er *m God*
Gras, ¨-er *n grass*
grell *flashy, garish*
großartig *great*
Großmutter, ¨ *f grandmother*
Großvater, ¨ *m grandfather*
grün *green*
Grundzahl, -en *f cardinal number*
gut *good; well*
Gute Nacht! *Good night!*
Gute Reise! *Have a good trip!*
Guten Abend! *Good evening!*
Guten Morgen! *Good morning!*
Guten Tag! *Good morning/afternoon!*

H

Haar, -e *n hair*
Haarbürste, -n *f hair brush*
haben *to have*
Hagel *m hail*
Hallo! *Hello!*
halten *to hold; to stop*
Hand, ¨-e *f hand*
Handtasche, -n *f handbag*
Handtuch, ¨-er *n towel*
Handy, -s *n mobile phone*
Happen, - *m mouthful*
Haus, ¨-er *n house, home*
Haustier, -e *n pet*
heiß *hot*
heiße Schokolade, -n *f hot chocolate*
helfen *to help*
hell *light*
hellblau *light/pale blue*
Hemd, -en *n shirt*
herausfinden *to find out*
herstellen *to manufacture, to produce*
herumfahren *to go (a)round*
heute *today*
hier *here*
Hilfe, -n *f help*
Himmel, - *m sky*
hingehen *to go (there)*
hinter *behind*
Hobby, -s *n hobby*
Hocker, - *m stool*
höflich *polite*
holen *to get*
Hölle, -n *f hell*
hören *to hear; to listen to*
Hose, -n *f trousers*
Hotel, -s *n hotel*
Hüfte, -n *f hip*

I

ich *I*
Illusion, -en *f illusion*
Illustration, -en *f illustration*
im *in the, into the; at the; on the*
in *in, into; at; on*
in Ordnung *all right, okay*
Ingenieur *m* / **Ingenieurin** *f engineer*
Innere *n inside*
ins Kino gehen *to go to the cinema*
ins Museum gehen *to go to museums*
interessant *interesting*
Interesse, -n *n interest*
Ire *m* / **Irin** *f Irishman / Irishwoman*

irisch *Irish*
Irland *Ireland*
irre *crazy*

J

ja *yes*
Jacke, -n *f* *jacket*
Jahr, -e *n* *year*
Januar *January*
je *ever*
jede(r, s) *each, every*
jemand *somebody, someone, anybody, anyone*
jetzt *now*
Job, -s *m* *job*
Juli *July*
Juni *June*

K

Kabel, - *m* *cable*
Kaffee, -s *m* *coffee*
Kajalstift, -e *m* *eyeliner*
Kalender, - *m* *calendar; diary*
kalt *cold*
Kanadier *m* / **Kanadierin** *f* *Canadian*
Kapitän, -e *m* *captain*
Karneval *m* *carnival*
Karotte, -n *f* *carrot*
Kartoffelbrei *m* *mashed potatoes*
Käse, - *m* *cheese*
Katze, -n *f* *cat*
kaufen *to buy*
Kaufhaus, ¨-er *n* *department store*
kein(e) *no*
kennen *to know*
kennenlernen *to meet, to get to know*
Kette, -n *f* *necklace*
Kind, -er *n* *child*
Kinn, -e *n* *chin*
Kirche, -n *f* *church*
Kirsche, -n *f* *cherry*
Kiwi, -s *f* *kiwi*
Klamotten *Pl* *gear*
Kleber, - *m* *glue*
Kleid, -er *n* *dress*
Kleidung, -en *f* *clothes*
klingeln *to ring the bell; to ring*
Knie, - *n* *knee*
Koch *m* / **Köchin** *f* *cook*
kochen *to cook*
Koffer, - *m* *suitcase*
Köln *Cologne*
kommen *to come*
Kommode, -n *f* *chest of drawers*
komplett *complete; completely*
Kondom, -e *n* *condom*
können *can, may, to be able to*
Kontakt, -e *m* *contact*
Kontaktdaten *Pl* *contact details*
Kopf, ¨-e *m* *head*
Kopfhörer, - *m* *headphones*
Kopfschmerzen *Pl* *headache*
Kopfschmerztablette, -n *f* *headache tablet*
Körperteil, -e *n* *part of the body*
Krankenhaus, ¨-er *n* *hospital*
Krass! *Wow!*
Krawatte, -n *f* *tie*
kreativ *creative; creatively*
kriminell *criminal*
Küche, -n *f* *kitchen*
Kühlschrank, ¨-e *m* *fridge*
Kulturtasche, -n *f* *toiletry bag*

L

Label, -s *n* *label*
Lachs, -e *m* *salmon*
Lampe, -n *f* *lamp*
Landwirtschaft *f* *agriculture*
lang *long; for*
langsam *slow; slowly*
sich **langweilen** *to be bored*
langweilig *boring, dull*
Laune, -n *f* *mood*
laut *loud*
leeren *to empty*
leidenschaftlich *passionate*
leider *I'm afraid, unfortunately*
lesen *to read*
Leute *Pl* *people*
Licht, -er *n* *Licht*
Lidschatten, - *m* *eyeshadow*
lieben *to love*
Liebesleben, - *n* *love life*
Liegestuhl, ¨-e *m* *deck chair*

lila *purple*
links *left*
Lippe, -n *f* *lip*
Lippenstift, -e *m* *lipstick*
Livemusik *f* *live music*
LKW, -s *m* *lorry*
Longdrink, -s *m* *long drink*
losmüssen *to have to be off*
lustig *funny*

M

machen *to make, to do*
Mädchen, - *n* *girl*
Magen, ¨-en *m* *stomach*
Mai *May*
mal *times*
man *one, you*
Mantel, ¨ *m* *coat*
März *March*
mehr *more*
mein(e) *my*
sich **melden** *to report; to get in touch*
Mensch, -en *m* *person*
Metzgerei, -en *f* *butcher's*
Milliarde, -n *f* *billion*
Million, -en *f* *million*
Minute, -n *f* *minute*
mit *with; by*
miteinander *together*
Mittag *m* *noon*
mittags *at noon*
Mittwoch *Wednesday*
Möbel *Pl* *furniture*
mögen *may, to like*
Möglichkeit, -en *f* *opportunity*
Monat, -e *m* *month*
Montag *Monday*
morgen *tomorrow*
Morgen, - *m* *morning*
morgens *in the morning*
Motorrad, ¨-er *n* *motorcycle*
müde *tired*
Müdigkeit *f* *tiredness*
Mund, ¨-er *m* *mouth*
Musik *f* *music*
müssen *to have to, must*
Mutter, ¨ *f* *mother*

N

nach *to; after; past*
nach Hause *home*
nächste(r, s) *next*
nächstes Mal *next time*
Nacht, ¨-e *f* *night*
Nachttisch, -e *m* *bedside table*
Nase, -n *f* *nose*
Nationalität, -en *f* *nationality*
neben *next to*
Neffe, -n *m* *nephew*
nein *no*
nett *nice*
neun *nine*
neunzehn *nineteen*
Neuseeländer *m* / **Neuseeländerin** *f*
New Zealander
nicht *not*
nicht wirklich *not really*
Nichte, -n *f* *niece*
nichts *nothing*
Nickerchen, - *n* *nap*
nie *never*
nieseln *to drizzle*
Nieselregen *m* *drizzle*
niesen *to sneeze*
noch *still*
noch etwas *some more*
noch mal *again*
noch nicht *not yet*
Nordsee *f* *North Sea*
Not, ¨-e *f* *need, poverty*
Notausgang, ¨-e *m* *emergency exit*
Notfall, ¨-e *m* *emergency*
November *November*
nüchtern *sober*
nur *just, only*

O

ob *whether, if*
Oberkörper, - *m* *upper body*
Obst *n* *fruit*
obwohl *although, though*
oder *or*
Ofen, Öfen *m* *oven*
oft *often*
Ohr, -en *n* *ear*

Ohrring, -e *m earring*
Oktober *October*
Oma, -s *f gran*
Onkel, - *m uncle*
Opa, -s *m grandpa*
orange *orange*
Ordnung, -en *f tidiness, order*
Ordnungszahl, -en *f ordinal number*
Orientierung, -en *f orientation*
orientierungslos *disoriented*
original *original*
Österreich *Austria*
Österreicher *m* / **Österreicherin** *f Austrian*
österreichisch *Austrian*

P

packen *to pack*
Panne, -n *f breakdown*
Paprika, -s *f pepper*
Pardon *Pardon*
Parfum, -s *n perfume*
Passagier, -e *m passenger*
passieren *to happen*
Penis, -se *m penis*
perfekt *perfect*
pflanzen *to plant*
Pflaume, -n *f plum*
Pilz, -e *m mushroom*
pinkeln *to pee*
planen *to plan*
Platz, ¨-e *m place, seat; room; square*
plötzlich *suddenly*
Po, -s *m bottom / bum*
Portemonnaie, -s *n wallet*
Priester, - *m priest*
professionell *professional*
Prominente(r) *celebrity*
Puppe, -n *f doll*

Q

quadratisch *square*

R

Rad, ¨-er *n wheel*
Rasierer, - *m shaver*
rauchen *to smoke*
rechts *right*
Rechtsanwalt *m* / **Rechtsanwältin** *f lawyer*
Regal, -e *n bookshelves*
Regen *m rain*
Regenbogen, - *m rainbow*
regnen *to rain*
Reinigung, -en *f dry cleaner's*
reisen *to travel*
Reisepass, ¨-e *m passport*
Reißverschluss, ¨-e *m zip*
rennen *to run*
Restaurant, -s *n restaurant*
reuevoll *full of remorse*
Rhein *the Rhine*
richtig *correct, right*
Richtung, -en *f direction*
riechen *to smell*
Ring, -e *m ring*
Rock, ¨-e *m skirt*
Rohrbruch, ¨-e *m burst pipe*
rosa *pink*
rot *red*
Rotwein, -e *m red wine*
Rouge, - *n blusher*
Rucksack, ¨-e *m backpack*
rückwärts *backwards*
rufen *to call*
ruhig *calm, quiet*
Rum, - *m rum*
rumhängen *to hang out*
rund *round*

S

Saft, ¨-e *m juice*
sagen *to say, to tell*
Samstag *Saturday*
sauber machen *to clean*
Schaden, ¨-en *m damage*
schauen *to look*
Schaufel, -n *f shovel*
Schauspieler *m* / **Schauspielerin** *f actor*
scheinen *to seem; to shine*
Scheinwerfer, - *m headlight*
Scheiße!/Kacke! *Shit!*
schicken *to send*
Schinken, - *m ham*

Schlafanzug, ¨-e *m* *pair of pyjamas*
schlafen *to sleep*
Schlafzimmer, - *n* *bedroom*
Schlange, -n *f* *snake*
schlecht *bad; sick*
Schlüssel, - *m* *key*
schmecken *to taste*
Schmerz, -en *m* *pain*
schmerzhaft *painful, sore*
Schmuck, - *m* *jewellery*
Schnaps, ¨-e *m* *schnapps*
Schnee *m* *snow*
schneien *to snow*
schnell *fast, quick, quickly*
schon *yet, already*
schön *nice*
Schorle, -n *f* *spritzer*
Schrank, ¨-e *m* *cupboard; wardrobe*
Schreck, -e *m* *fear*
schrecklich *horrible*
Schreibtisch, -e *m* *desk*
Schuh, -e *m* *shoe*
Schulbildung *f* *(school) education*
Schulter, -n *f* *shoulder*
schütten *to pour down*
schwarz *black*
Schweiz *f* *Switzerland*
Schweizer *m /* **Schweizerin** *f* *Swiss*
schweizerisch *Swiss*
schwer *heavy; hard, difficult*
schwierig *difficult, hard*
schwimmen *to swim*
sechs *six*
sechzehn *sixteen*
sechzig *sixty*
sehen *to see*
sehr *very*
Seife, -n *f* *soap*
sein *to be*
sein(e) *his; its*
selbstständig *self-employed*
Sellerie, - *m* *celery*
September *September*
Sessel, - *m* *armchair*
Shampoo, -s *n* *shampoo*
Shorts *Pl* *pair of shorts*
sich *herself; himself; itself; oneself; themselves; yourself; yourselves*
sieben *seven*
siebzehn *seventeen*
signalisieren *to signal*
singen *to sing*
Sitz, -e *m* *seat*
sitzen *to sit*
so *so; like that, like this*
Socke, -n *f* *sock*
Sofa, -s *n* *sofa*
sofort *immediately, at once*
Sohn, ¨-e *m* *son*
Soldat *m /* **Soldatin** *f* *soldier*
sollen *shall*
somit *consequently, therefore*
Sonne, -n *f* *sun*
Sonnenbrille, -n *f* *sunglasses*
Sonnencreme, -s *f* *sun cream*
Sonntag *Sunday*
sonst *otherwise*
sonst noch *else*
soviel *as far as; so much*
später *later*
Spiegel, - *m* *mirror*
spielen *to play*
Sport *m* *sport*
sprechen *to speak, to talk*
Spüle, -n *f* *sink*
Stammtisch, -e *m* *table reserved for the regulars*
staubsaugen *to vacuum, to hoover®*
Staubsauger, - *m* *vacuum cleaner*
Steckdose, -n *f* *socket*
Stecker, - *m* *plug*
stehlen *to steal*
Stelle, -n *f* *place*
stellen *to put*
sterben *to die*
Sternzeichen, - *n* *sign of the zodiac*
stimmen *to be right*
stinkend *stinking*
Stirn, -en *f* *forehead*
stockbesoffen *dead drunk*
Stockwerk, -e *n* *floor*
stören *to bother, to disturb*
Stoßstange, -n *f* *bumper*
Stratosphäre *f* *stratosphere*
Strumpfhose, -n *f* *tights*

Stuhl, ¨-e *m* *chair*
Sturm, ¨-e *m* *storm*
stürmen *to blow a gale*
stürmisch *stormy*
suchen *to look for*
Supermarkt, ¨-e *m* *supermarket*
Suppe, -n *f* *soup*

T

Tag, -e *m* *day*
Taille, -n *f* *waist*
Tampon, -s *m* *tampon*
Tandem, -s *n* *tandem*
tanken *to get petrol*
Tante, -n *f* *aunt*
tanzen *to dance*
tauchen *to dive*
tauschen *to exchange, to swap*
Tee, -s *m* *tea*
Telefon, -e *n* *phone, telephone*
Telefonnummer, -n *f* *telephone number*
Temperatur, -en *f* *temperature*
Teppich, -e *m* *rug; carpet*
Theater, - *n* *theatre*
Tierheim, -e *n* *animal shelter*
Tisch, -e *m* *table*
Tischtennis *n* *table tennis*
Tochter, ¨ *f* *daughter*
Toilette, -n *f* *toilet*
Toll! *Awesome!*
Tomate, -n *f* *tomato*
tot *dead*
total *absolutely*
traurig *sad*
treffen *to meet*
treten *to step*
trinken *to drink*
Trompete, -n *f* *trumpet*
Tschüs(s)! *Bye!*
T-Shirt, -s *n* *T-shirt*
Tube, -n *f* *tube*
tun *to do*
Tür, -en *f* *door*
Typ, -en *m* *guy; type*

U

U-Bahn, -en *f* *underground*
über *over*
übermorgen *the day after tomorrow*
Uhrzeit, -en *f* *time of day*
um *at; round*
umkehren *to turn around*
unabhängig *independent*
unangenehm *unpleasant*
und *and*
und zwar *in fact, actually*
unglaublich *incredible*
unter *under*
Unterhose, -n *f* *underpants*
Unterkörper, - *m* *lower body*
Unterwäsche, - *f* *underwear*
urkomisch *screamingly funny*
Ursache, -n *f* *cause*

V

Vater, ¨ *m* *father*
verantwortlich *responsible*
verboten *forbidden*
verbunden *connected*
Verdammt! *Damn!*
Verdammte Scheiße! *Bloody hell!*
vergessen *to forget*
Verkehrsmittel, - *n* *means of transport*
verlassen *to leave*
verrückt *mad*
verschicken *to send off*
versehentlich *inadvertent; by mistake*
verstecken *to hide*
Versuch, -e *m* *attempt*
verwirrt *confused*
viel *much, plenty of, a lot of*
vier *four*
vierzehn *fourteen*
vierzig *forty*
violett *violet*
völlig *absolutely, completely*
von *of; about; by; from*
vor *in front of; before; to; ago*
vorgestern *the day before yesterday*
vorher *before*
vorwärts *forwards*
VW-Bus, -se *m* *VW camper van*

W

wagen *to venture, to dare*
wahr *true*
Wald, ⸚er *m* *forest*
Wange, -n *f* *cheek*
wann *when, whenever*
warm *warm*
warten *to wait*
warum *why*
Was ist los? *What's the matter?*
Waschbecken, - *n* *sink*
Wasser, - *n* *water*
Wechselgeld, - *n* *change*
weg *off, away*
Weihnachten, - *n* *Christmas*
weil *because*
Weile, - *f* *while*
Wein, -e *m* *wine*
weiß *white*
Weißwein, -e *m* *white wine*
Weltraumforschung *f* *space research*
wenn *if; when*
wer *who*
werden *to become; shall, will*
Wette, -n *f* *bet*
Wetter, - *n* *weather*
Whisky, -s *m* *whisky*
wie *as; how; like*
Wie geht es Ihnen? *How are you? (formal)*
Wie geht's? *How are you?*
Wie wäre es mit ...? *What about ...?*
wieder *again*
wiedersehen *to see again*
wild *wild*
Willkommen! *Welcome!*
Wimper, -n *f* *Wimper*
Wimperntusche, -n *f* *mascara*
Wind, -e *m* *wind*
windig *windy*
Windstille *f* *calm*
Wir sehen uns! *See you!*
wirklich *really; actually*
wissen *to know*
wo *where*
Woche, -n *f* *week*
Wochenende, -n *n* *weekend*
Wochenmarkt, ⸚e *m* *weekly market*
Wochentag, -e *m* *day of the week*
Wodka, -s *m* *vodka*
woher *where ... from*
wohnen *to live, to stay*
Wohnung, -en *f* *apartment, flat*
Wohnzimmer, - *n* *living room*
Wolke, -n *f* *cloud*
wollen *to want*
wunderbar *wonderful*
wunderschön *beautiful*
Würstchen, - *n* *sausage*
wütend *angry*

Z

zahlen *to pay*
Zahnbürste, -n *f* *toothbrush*
Zahnpasta *f* *toothpaste*
Zeh, -en *m* *toe*
zehn *ten*
zehntausend *ten thousand*
Zeitangabe, -n *f* *expression of time*
ziemlich *quite*
zu *to; too*
zu Hause *at home*
zu sein *to be shut*
zu viel *too much*
zunehmend *increasing; increasingly*
zurück *back*
zwanzig *twenty*
zwei *two*
zwölf *twelve*